W9-ADZ-010

The U.S.
Marine Corps
and Military Careers

R. Conrad Stein

Enslow Publishers, Inc.
40 Industrial Road
Box 398
Berkeley Heights, NJ 07922
USA

http://www.enslow.com

HOWARD COUNTY LIBRARY
BIG SPRING, TEXAS

Copyright © 2006 by R. Conrad Stein

All rights reserved.

No part of this book may be reproduced by any means without the written permission of the publisher.

Library of Congress Cataloging-in-Publication Data

Stein, R. Conrad.
    The U.S. Marine Corps and military careers / R. Conrad Stein.
      p. cm. — (The U.S. Armed Forces and military careers)
    Includes bibliographical references and index.
    ISBN-10: 0-7660-2521-7 (library edition)
    ISBN-10: 0-7660-3263-9 (paperback edition)
    1. United States. Marine Corps—Juvenile literature. 2. United States. Marine Corps—Vocational guidance—Juvenile literature. I. Title. II. Series.
    VE23.S74 2006
    359.9'602373—dc22   2005037881

ISBN-13: 978-0-7660-2521-9 (library edition)
ISBN-13: 978-0-7660-3263-7 (paperback edition)

Printed in the United States of America

10 9 8 7 6 5 4 3 2

To Our Readers: We have done our best to make sure that all Internet Addresses in this book were active and appropriate when we went to press. However, the author and publisher have no control over and assume no liability for the material available on those Internet sites or on other Web sites they may link to. Any comments or suggestions can be sent by e-mail to comments@enslow.com or to the address on the back cover.

Illustration Credits: AFP/Getty Images, pp. 43, 116 (bottom); ©Corel Corporation, pp. 31, 37, 115 (bottom), 116 (top); The Library of Congress, pp. 20, 115 (top); National Archives and Records Administration, pp. 12, 14, 17, 114; R. Conrad Stein, p. 113; Time Life Pictures/Getty Images, pp. 40, 116 (middle); U.S. Department of Defense, pp. 57, 121 (bottom); U.S. Marine Corps, pp. 26, 28, 29, 58. 68, 70, 71, 98, 115 (middle), 122 (bottom); U.S. Marine Corps, illustration by Lance Corporal Jeffrey A. Cosola, p. 41; U.S. Marine Corps, photo by Chief Photographer's Mate Johnny Bivera, pp. 2 (middle), 6; U.S. Marine Corps, photo by Corporal Adam C. Schnell, p. 109; U.S. Marine Corps, photo by Corporal Chris Flurry, p. 60; U.S. Marine Corps, photo by Corporal Julie A. Paynter, p. 51; U.S. Marine Corps, photo by Corporal Matthew J. Apprendi, p. 50; U.S. Marine Corps, photo by Corporal Matthew R. Jones, p. 111; U.S. Marine Corps, photo by Corporal Robert A. Sturkie, p. 8; U.S. Marine Corps, photo by Corporal Susan Smith, p. 94; U.S. Marine Corps, photo by Corporal Thomas Perry, p. 65; U.S. Marine Corps, photo by Corporal Rich Mattingly, p. 93; U.S. Marine Corps, photo by Gunnery Sergeant Kent Flora, p. 102 U.S. Marine Corps, photo by Lance Corporal Dorian Gardner, pp. 3, 67, 121 (top); U.S. Marine Corps, photo by Lance Corporal Hugh S. Holder III, p. 46; U.S. Marine Corps, photo by Lance Corporal Miguel A. Carrasco, Jr., pp. 1, 75; U.S. Marine Corps, photo by Pfc. Regina N. Ortiz, p. 107; U.S. Marine Corps, photo by PH1 Martin Maddock, pp. 2 (right), 79; U.S. Marine Corps, Private First Class Michael S. Cifuentes, p. 77; U.S. Marine Corps, photo by Sergeant Brandon O'Brien, p. 54; U.S. Marine Corps, photo by Sergeant G. S. Thomas, p. 7; U.S. Marine Corps, Sergeant Jemssy Alvarez, Jr., p. 83; U.S. Marine Corps, photo by Sergeant Jerad W. Alexander, p. 104; U.S. Marine Corps, photo by Sergeant Joseph R. Chenelly, pp. 2 (left), 4, 86, 117; U.S. Marine Corps, photo by Sergeant Luis R. Agostini, pp. 52, 121 (middle); U.S. Marine Corps, photo by Sergeant Stephen M. DeBoard, p. 90; U.S. Marine Corps, photo by Staff Sergeant F. B. Zimmerman, pp. 72, 122 (top); U.S. Marine Corps, photo by Staff Sergeant J. L. Wright, Jr., p. 63.

Cover Illustration: R. Conrad Stein (back cover); U.S. Marine Corps, photo by Sergeant Joseph R. Chenelly (front cover).

Contents

▲ On November 25, 2001, Marines from the 15th Marine Expeditionary Unit move to a new position in Afghanistan after seizing an enemy base. The man in front is carrying shoulder-launched missiles.

First to Fight

September 11, 2001, is a day burned into the memory of all Americans. On that day, two hijacked jetliners slammed into the twin towers of New York's World Trade Center, bursting into flames on impact. Another captured passenger jet crashed into the Pentagon in Washington, D.C. Still another hijacked aircraft went down in rural Pennsylvania. Almost three thousand people were killed on September 11.

Orchestrating this incredible act of terrorism was a shadowy group called al Qaeda. The group was led by a Saudi Arabian man named Osama bin Laden. Al Qaeda and Bin Laden were headquartered in the Asian country of Afghanistan. Days after the attack, American special forces flew to Afghanistan and began the hunt for Bin Laden. In late November, the first regular troops landed in the remote country. Those regulars were U.S. Marines. The mission was not unusual for the

5

Marines. One Marine slogan is: "First to Fight." In almost every war in American history, the Marines were the first troops sent into action.

Afghanistan is a dry, mountainous country where warfare has been a part of life for hundreds of years. Marine helicopters loaded with ground troops landed in the lonely Afghan mountains. The Marines began looking for Bin Laden and members of al Qaeda. They searched villages and explored caves that could be used as hideouts. Above the

▲ Marines ride in a CH-46E Sea Knight helicopter on their way to their mission in Afghanistan in December 2001.

men on foot flew helicopters and jet planes of the Marine Air Wing. Hunting down the terrorists was dangerous work. Days after their landing, a Marine stepped on a land mine while his platoon patrolled near a village. One Marine lost a leg and another suffered a severe head injury.

The Afghan operation was a frustrating experience for the Marines and the other military services deployed there. Many of the Marines in the country were teenagers. By December 2005, American forces had lost 259 lives, including at least 25 Marines, and they had yet to find Osama bin Laden.

First Lieutenant Charles E. Hayter lost the bottom part of his right leg to a land mine while in Afghanistan. Despite being injured, he returned to the country after recovering to lead his platoon.

A firefight broke out on June 26, 2004. The brief battle was given scant attention in American newspapers; however, two Marines were killed. Names of the two young men were not immediately released, pending notification to their families. A military spokesman in Washington said, "Two Marines were killed and one was

▲ A Marine removes a rocket-propelled grenade that he found in a cave in Afghanistan on April 30, 2004. The Taliban and al Qaeda often hide weapons in the many caves in the mountains of Afghanistan.

wounded during an operation northeast of Asadabad [in eastern Afghanistan]."[1]

The Americans succeeded in driving the Afghan government, called the Taliban, out of power. For years the Taliban had allowed al Qaeda to use Afghanistan as their base of operations. With the fall of the Taliban, Bin Laden was at least on the run. And the U.S. Marines continued to pursue him. A bumper sticker seen on vehicles at many Marine bases in the United States reads:

> *It's God's Job to Forgive Bin Laden.*
> *It's Our Job to Arrange the Meeting.*[2]

Who are these men and women who call themselves U.S. Marines? Sometimes they are known as "soldiers of the sea" because they often ride Navy ships into battle. "Soldiers of the sea" is no longer an entirely proper name. Today's Marine units are frequently airlifted to their duty sites. Landlocked Afghanistan, for example, is nine hundred miles from the nearest seacoast.

Whether they travel by air or the sea, the Marine Corps has a long and proud history of serving the United States. Men and women of the United States Marine Corps (USMC) abide by an old message that sums up their spirit: "The Marines have landed; the situation is well at hand."

Two

The Few, the Proud: the Marines

Resolved, That two battalions of marines be raised . . . that they be inlisted and commissioned to serve for and during the present war between Great Britain and the colonies . . .[1]

—Language from the enabling act which gave birth to the Marine Corps on November 10, 1775

The Beginnings

The Marine Corps is actually older than the nation it serves. The Corps was created on November 10, 1775, by an act of the Second Continental Congress. At the time, the United States was just beginning its war of independence against Great Britain. November 10 is now celebrated as the official Marine Corps birthday. The word "Corps" in Marine Corps is pronounced *core*. Many Marines will shorten the term "Marine Corps" by dropping the word "Marine" and saying,

"I serve in the Corps." The first official Marine unit was formed in December 1775 at a Philadelphia inn called Tun Tavern. That outfit consisted of one hundred men, all of whom were volunteers.

Using marines as sea soldiers was a tradition that dated back to the British navy. In sea battles, British marine sharpshooters climbed into the riggings of sailing ships and fired down at sailors on enemy vessels. The sharpshooters took special aim at enemy officers.

Saltier Than Thou

Among themselves, Marines enjoy bragging about their "saltiness," meaning how much time they have served in the Corps. One old story says, "I'm so salty that when the Lord said 'Let there be light' I was the guy who turned them on." Bragging rights for the saltiest of all belong to Lieutenant John Watson. In May 1775, Watson joined a Massachusetts ship as the first Marine ever to report for duty. He is, of course, the saltiest old salt in the history of the Corps.

British marines also disembarked from ships, rowed to hostile shores, and engaged in land warfare. A third duty of British marines was to act as a police force over sailors by breaking up mutinies. This unpleasant part of their duty bred a resentment between marines and sailors, which to a certain extent carried over to the American military.

On March 3, 1776, a U.S. ship called the *Alfred* landed a small force of Marines on New Providence Island in the Bahamas. At the time, war raged between the United States and its mother country, Great Britain. New Providence Island was a British stronghold. After thirteen days of combat, the Marines overwhelmed British soldiers on the island while capturing two forts and seizing eighty-eight

▲ In March 1776, Marines row toward the U.S.S. *Alfred* after capturing Britain's Fort Montague on New Providence Island in the Bahamas.

enemy cannons. The ship-to-shore operation at New Providence Island was the first amphibious landing performed by the USMC.

The United States gained its independence from Great Britain in 1783. As an infant nation, it was weak and subject to intimidation by foreign powers. One such foreign group was the Barbary Pirates who were headquartered in North Africa. In 1803, President Thomas Jefferson sent Navy vessels and several hundred Marines to North Africa. They were ordered to subdue the pirate bands who were attacking American ships. The Marines were led by Lieutenant Presley N. O'Bannon. First, the Marines had to march some six hundred miles over the scorching North African desert to reach a pirate-held fort in the state of Tripoli. There, O'Bannon and his men launched a bold attack in 1805. After a harsh battle, the Marines defeated the pirates. For the first time ever, the American flag flew above shores on the opposite side of the Atlantic Ocean. Also, the Marines gained the second line of their hymn: ". . . To the shores of Tripoli."

A new conflict called the War of 1812 broke out between Great Britain and the United States. In August 1814, the Americans suffered the ultimate embarrassment when a British army stormed their capital, Washington, D.C., and burned down the city's prominent buildings. Poorly trained and poorly equipped American troops fled before the professional British soldiers who marched on the capital. Only a small unit of sailors and Marines put up spirited

APRIL 27 1805 AFTER A BOMBARDMENT OF DERNE TRIPOLI BY THE HORNET NAUTILUS AND ARGUS A LANDING PARTY WITH LIEUTENANT OBANNON OF THE MARINES IN COMMAND HAULED DOWN THE TRIPOLITAN FLAG AND HOISTED OLD GLORY FOR THE FIRST TIME OVER A FORT IN THE OLD WORLD

▲ O'Bannon's Marines raised the American flag after capturing a fort on Tripoli.

resistance against the British onslaught.

In the Mexican-American War (1846–1848), Marines made landings on the Atlantic and the Pacific coasts of Mexico. A Marine unit was first to enter the city gates of Mexico City. In September 1847, the Marines hoisted the Stars and Stripes over the National Palace (later called the Halls of Montezuma) in the Mexican capital. Montezuma was once the leader of the Aztec people in Mexico. By taking the National Palace, the words "From the Halls of Montezuma" were added to the "Marine hymn."

Throughout the 1850s, the burning issue of slavery split the United States into two hostile camps. In October 1859, an antislavery zealot named John Brown took over a government arsenal at Harpers Ferry, Virginia. Brown and his small band of followers urged slaves to rise up in rebellion and join him at the arsenal. Once more, Marines were the first troops to arrive on the scene. A Marine unit broke into the firehouse the group had

The "Marine Hymn"

The "Marine Hymn" is the oldest official song of any of the U.S. services. Tradition says the first two lines of the "Marine Hymn" were written in the 1840s by a Marine on duty in the Mexican-American War. The melody came later and was taken from a French opera called *Genevieve de Brabant*. Here is the first stanza of the "Marine Hymn":

*From the Halls of Montezuma
To the shores of Tripoli;
We will fight our country's battles
In the air, on land and sea;
First to fight for right and freedom
And to keep our honor clean;
We are proud to claim the title
of United States Marine.*

NOTE: The original words to the fourth line of the Hymn were: "On the land as on the sea." The words were changed to "In the air, on land, and sea" after World War II when Marine aviation became prominent.

converted into a fort and captured John Brown. The Marines were led by Army Colonel Robert E. Lee, who later became a brilliant commander of the Southern forces. The Harpers Ferry raid was one of the events that fueled the start of the Civil War (1861–1865).

The Civil War divided the Marine Corps as it did the nation. About half of the men of the Corps resigned to fight with Confederate forces. Marines loyal to the Union served in sea battles at New Orleans and at Mobile Bay.

Service in the Small Wars

After the Civil War, many government leaders considered abolishing the Marine Corps. They believed Army troops could readily take over Marine duties. Still others argued that sea soldiers working closely with the Navy were needed to fight the "small wars" that often broke out in far-off ports. Finally, the government decided to keep the Marine Corps, although at minimum strength.

So-called small wars in the late 1800s and early 1900s kept the Corps on fighting fronts all over the globe. Marine units landed more than a dozen times on the coast of China to put down rebellions that threatened American interests. Men of the Corps performed similar missions in Panama, Nicaragua, and Haiti. Minor conflicts in Latin countries were sometimes called "banana wars." Some modern historians have cited the banana-war period as an example of the United States bullying its neighbors in Latin America.

In the Spanish-American War (fought between April and August 1898), Marines again were the first to fight. Marines were the first Americans to land in Cuba and the first to storm the shores of

▲ Marines on patrol in Haiti in 1919

the Philippines. Marines also occupied the former Spanish territories of Guam and Puerto Rico.

Men of the USMC faced grave dangers in the small wars of the early 1900s. They flushed deadly snipers from unseen positions and fought pitched battles with rebels. The men worked under the broiling sun while suffering tropical diseases such as malaria. Some rose to tasks beyond their duties. In 1915, Sergeant Dan Daly fought in Haiti. While under fire, he pulled a submerged machine gun from a mountain stream. Daly's actions earned him the Medal of Honor, the highest award given to a United States service person. It was Daly's second such honor. Sergeant Dan Daly remains the only Marine-enlisted man to ever receive two Medals of Honor. Smedley D. Butler, who served as a Marine officer in the banana-war period, also was given the nation's highest award twice.

Marines in the Great War

In August 1914, World War I began in Europe. Military leaders believed the conflict would be short-lived. In its beginnings, the war appealed to European patriotism. Soldiers marched out of villages while bands played and neighbors cheered. No one imagined the battlefield effect of new weapons such as machine guns and fast-firing artillery. World War I ground down to static, ugly trench warfare. Huge armies fought each other from trenches separated by scarred ground often just a football field in length. In the mud of those long ditches, the pride of European youth bled and died.

The United States entered World War I in April 1917 when Congress declared war on Germany. Upon arriving at the battlegrounds, Marines and army troops encountered the same grim trenches where Europeans had fought for years. Like the Europeans, the Americans lived in the muddy ditches along with rats and swarms of insects.

Amphibious warfare, the Marine specialty, was not employed by the Corps in World War I. Instead, the Marines were used as regular infantry. They often served under army field officers. In combat, all American forces faced murderous artillery, poison gas, and deadly machine guns. In the summer of 1918, a fresh group of Marines occupied a trench line just in time to meet a German offensive. A French colonel suggested the Marines retreat rather than confront the advancing Germans. To this suggestion the Marine commander reportedly said, "Retreat, hell! We just got here."[2]

In June 1918, the Fourth Marine brigade attacked a German-held forest named Belleau Wood. During this storied battle, the young men discovered the mind-numbing horror of war. Veteran German machine gunners rained deadly fire on the Marines. In one day, the men of the Corps suffered eleven hundred killed or wounded.[3] This one-day figure at Belleau Wood was greater than the total number of casualties the Marines had endured in their entire previous history. Still the Marines

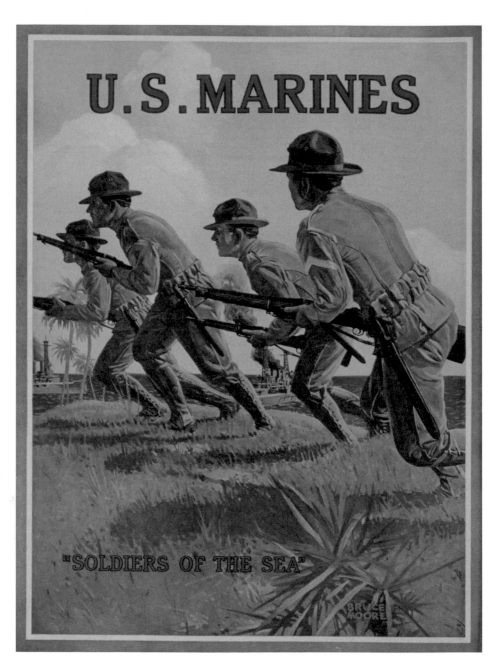

▲ This poster encouraged men to join the Marines during World War I.

triumphed. German soldiers were so impressed with the fighting skills of these special American troops that they called them *Teufel Hunden*, German for Devil Dogs.

World War I ended with the armistice signed November 11, 1918. Though the war was a violent part of American history, two Marine firsts occurred during the war years. On August 13, 1918, Opha Mae Johnson became the first woman Marine. During World War I, several hundred women served in the Corps, performing mainly secretarial duties. Women service in the Marines was discontinued after the World War I. In July 1918, the 1st Marine Aviation Air Force began operations in France. Marine pilots had trained in naval aviation schools earlier, but the World War I unit was the true beginning of Marine aviation.

At first, the bloody clash of arms of World War I was called the Great War due to its vastness and the terrible number of people killed. It was

Nicknames

Through the years the Marines have acquired several often-used nicknames:

Devil Dogs—The German name of respect given the Marines in World War I.

Gyrenes—The source of this term is obscure, but it was once used by British marines. The Corps picked up the nickname during the World War I years.

Jarheads—This term comes from a uniform that was used in the 19th century and had a collar so high it appeared the Marine's head was screwed into his neck.

Leathernecks—This stems from the leather collar Marines wore back in the 1800s. It is generally believed the leather collar uniform protected a man's neck during a sword fight.

Seagoing Bell Hops—This is a nickname not liked by Marines. It refers to units who wear their dress blue uniforms while guarding the Navy's finest ships. The uniform reminds some people of those of hotel employees.

also called the "war to end all wars" because it was generally thought humankind would never again be so foolish to enter a war of similar dimensions. But history soon wrote a sad message to those who believed the carnage of World War I would end all wars.

Hell in the Pacific

My heart pounded inside whenever I saw a buddy get hit and even more so when they died. We were taught to carry on and we knew we could not stop and dwell on the tragedy around us.[1]

—Robert Jones, a Marine
veteran of the Pacific War

Island Warfare

The rain of Japanese bombs that fell on Pearl Harbor on December 7, 1941, propelled the United States into World War II. It was a two-region war with U.S. forces operating in Europe and the Pacific. The Marines fought almost exclusively in the Pacific theater. There, the Marines were in the forefront of an island campaign. Island battles called upon their special skills in waging ship-to-shore warfare. American strategists viewed the Pacific islands as stepping stones or as rungs of a ladder. Each island conquered served as an advanced base. Airfields and supply dumps were built on the islands. The conquest of every new island was a new step on the march to Japan.

No other branch of the armed forces was so well trained and well equipped for amphibious warfare as were the Marines. Beginning in the 1920s, General John Lejeune insisted the Corps return to its roots as soldiers of the sea. Just before World War II, General Howland Smith supervised training exercises that saw large Marine units assault beaches. Two new landing craft were developed during the practice maneuvers. The Higgins boat was a flat-bottomed craft that held twenty to thirty assault troops. Men climbed from ships onto Higgins boats, which then took them to an enemy beach. Another landing craft, the amphibious tractor, had tank-like treads and was able to climb up the hostile beach.

Furious combat took place on the Pacific islands. Japanese soldiers served under a code called *bushido*, or "way of the warrior." To them, death in battle was acceptable, even glorious. Surrender, on the other hand, was an unthinkable disgrace. For more than three years, Marines landed on the hostile shores of islands held by these fanatical defenders. With the sea at their backs, the Marines had no choice but to move forward against an enemy pledged to kill them or die in the attempt. Young men barely out of high school fought and died over specks of land they had never heard of before—Guadalcanal, Tarawa, Kwajelein, Saipan, Tinian, Peleliu, Iwo Jima, Okinawa.

World War II was the coming-of-age for the Marine Corps. By 1944, more than 475,000 men and women served in the USMC. The American public hailed the Marines as elite infantry troops who were given the toughest job of the war. Hollywood churned out movies celebrating Marine heroism. But those fighting in the Pacific found no glamour in the war. They saw island battlefields strewn with bodies, all bloated and rotting under the tropical sun. In the jungles of the South Pacific, thousands of Marines contracted malaria and other tropical diseases. The sights, smells, and terror of island fighting stayed locked in men's minds for years afterward.

The First Step

From the deck of a ship, Guadalcanal looked lush and green. The small island was ringed by a silvery white beach. It seemed to be everyone's idea of a Pacific paradise. Eleven thousand Leathernecks splashed ashore in August 1942. There, they discovered the hidden horrors of Guadalcanal—spiders the size of golf balls, nightmarish looking land crabs, beetles as big as a man's thumb, and ferocious white ants whose bite stung like a needle.

The Japanese were building an airstrip on Guadalcanal. To drive the Marines off the island, they launched furious counterattacks by sea, land, and air.

CAREER PROFILE

John Basilone of New Jersey

In a frantic Guadalcanal battle in October 1943, Sergeant John Basilone of Raritan, New Jersey, kept firing his machine gun even though he was surrounded by attacking Japanese. When the machine gun overheated and failed to fire, Basilone held the enemy back by shooting his pistol. For his actions, Basilone was awarded the Medal of Honor. He was also sent back to the United States to participate in parades and other events designed to promote the war effort. Basilone soon felt guilty about being at home while his friends remained in the Pacific, and he asked to return to the fighting fronts. His request was granted, and Sergeant Basilone was killed in 1945 when his Marine unit attacked Iwo Jima. A statue in his hometown honors his memory.

Warships sailing off the beaches poured shell after shell on Marine positions. Enemy planes dropped bombs. On the rain-swept night of September 12, thousands of Japanese soldiers charged the Marines. The Americans fought back with machine guns, light artillery, rifles, bayonets, and even rocks and clubs. Marine lines held. But the morning after the battle, the island smelled of blood and death.

The Central Pacific

No other invasion symbolized the deadly nature of World War II amphibious operations more than Tarawa. The tiny island of Betio, the main target of the Tarawa chain, is surrounded by a coral reef. Marines landed on the island in November 1943. Some of their landing craft were amphibious tractors, called amtracs. The amtracs crawled over the coral propelled by their tank-like treads. But many landing boats were Higgins boats and were not equipped with treads. Those on board the Higgins boats had to jump out and wade through a lagoon while enemy machine guns blazed away at them. The waters turned pink with their blood. A sailor looking at the invasion through binoculars wrote, "Those poor guys plodding in chest-high water and getting shot down. I tried not to look, but I couldn't turn away. The horror of it hypnotized me."[2]

The Battle of Tarawa lasted only seventy-six hours, but it constituted slaughter on an unimaginable scale.[3] Marine casualties totaled 1,027 killed and twice that number wounded.[4] Months later, movies of American dead floating like logs in the lagoon were played in theaters in the United States. It marked the first time in World War II that films showed large numbers of American dead. The movie showings were ordered by President Franklin Roosevelt. The president wanted the public to realize the sacrifice of their armed forces. Many people left the movie houses in tears.

Peleliu was another island hell. The conquest of this island began in September 1944 and was expected to take several days. Instead, the fighting dragged on for weeks. Marine Corporal Eugene Sledge was a twenty year old who participated in the invasion. Sledge later wrote a powerful memoir called *With the Old Breed at Peleliu and Okinawa*. Though he was a brave and dedicated Marine,

▲ A Marine uses a flamethrower to clear a path through the thick jungle on Tarawa Island.

Sledge told of a moment on Peleliu when weeks and weeks of intense combat finally overwhelmed him:

> I felt myself choking up . . . I began sobbing. The harder I tried to stop the worse it got. My body shuddered and shook. Tears flowed out of my scratchy eyes. I was sickened and revolted to see healthy young men get hurt and killed day after day. I felt I couldn't take it anymore.[5]

The Navajo Code-talkers

Throughout the Pacific War, the Japanese tried to intercept American radio messages so they could anticipate their enemy's moves. Americans radioed in code, but the Japanese were skilled code-breakers. To counter Japanese intercepts, the Marines used Navajo Indians to relay orders by radio. Navajo is a complicated language spoken by only a few dozen people outside the tribe. The Marines gathered about four hundred enlisted men of Navajo descent and let them convey messages. They were sometimes called "windtalkers." The Navajos converted their ancient language to conform to military terms: besh-lo (ironfish) meant submarine and chay-da-gahi (tortoise) meant tank. Navajo words baffled the Japanese. No message intercepted was understood by the enemy as long as it was broadcast by Navajo Leathernecks.

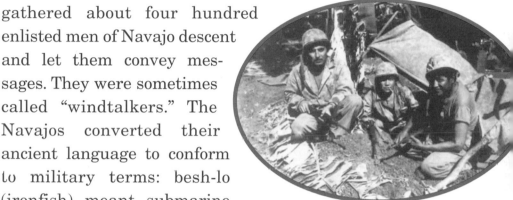

▲ Navajo code talkers of the South Pacific.

Iwo Jima

On February 19, 1945, a huge fleet of American warships surrounded the tiny treeless island of Iwo Jima. Battleships, cruisers, and destroyers opened up with their big guns. The island disappeared under a cloud of exploding shells. At 7:30 in the morning, scores of landing craft, each crowded with up to twenty Marines, churned toward Iwo Jima. At the beach, ramps opened and the Marines charged out. At first, Japanese defenders held their fire. Then, with terrifying suddenness, artillery shells and machine-gun bullets screamed at the Marines. Desperately the Americans inched forward, crawling on their bellies like snakes. In minutes, twisted bodies of dead men lay sprawled on the sand. Wounded men shrieked in agony.

The furious battle for Iwo Jima raged day and night. On the morning of the fifth day, the Marines fought their way up Mount Suribachi, the ancient volcano that dominated the island. At the peak of the mountain they found a pipe they could use as a staff and they raised an American flag. Men below cheered at the sight of the Stars and Stripes waving in the wind. Ships offshore blew their whistles. It was determined the first flag was too small. So a runner was sent to fetch a larger flag, and five Marines and a Navy medic raised the new banner. Newspaperman Joe Rosenthal photographed this second flag-raising. Rosenthal had no idea he had taken the most famous photo of World War II.

The Battle of Iwo Jima lasted thirty-four days. Final victory came at a staggering cost in American blood: twenty-six thousand casualties including six thousand eight hundred dead.[6] Survivors of the battle were left almost paralyzed from horror and sheer exhaustion. Some Marines went insane due to the intense combat pressure.

The Marine Corps War Memorial

At the time of Iwo Jima, the United States had been at war for more than three years. The public was

The Marine Corps War Memorial in Washington, D.C., commemorates the raising of an American flag during the battle on Iwo Jima.

war-weary. Then the dramatic picture of Marines raising the flag on a bleak mountaintop thrilled the people and boosted their morale. The photo became a part of the American memory forever. On November 10, 1954, President Dwight Eisenhower dedicated the Marine Corps War Memorial in Washington, D.C. An inscription on the base of the monument repeats the words of Admiral Chester W. Nimitz, who said of the fighting men on Iwo Jima, "Uncommon Valor was a Common Virtue."

CAREER PROFILE

Lieutenant General Pedro A. del Valle (1893–1978)

Born in San Juan, Puerto Rico, Pedro del Valle graduated from the U.S. Naval Academy and was commissioned a Marine Lieutenant in 1915. He became an artillery expert, but he often led infantry troops. On Okinawa, he commanded the 1st Marine Division. In this capacity, he lived on the front lines with his men and faced the same dangers they faced. For his exceptional leadership on Okinawa, General del Valle was given the Distinguished Service Medal.

Okinawa

Okinawa was the final island, the last rung on the ladder stretching to Japan. On April 1, 1945, Marines and Army troops landed, all of them believing this would be a ghastly fight. To everyone's surprise, the Americans quickly conquered the northern two thirds of the island. Then the real fight took place in the south. Okinawa proved to be the bloodiest battle of the Pacific war. Marines and army troops served side by side trying to blast the Japanese defenders out of their caves and bunkers. At sea, naval ships suffered repeated attacks from kamikazes, the dreaded Japanese suicide bombers.

No one on the bloody island of Okinawa was aware that a super-secret operation called the Manhattan Project had given the United States the atomic bomb. At the time, Japan was an exhausted and virtually defeated nation. Some American leaders doubted the wisdom of using this powerful bomb on an already beaten nation. But the awful bloodletting on Iwo Jima and Okinawa erased all doubts. If U.S. forces had to invade the Japanese home islands, the casualties could have been terrible. On August 6, 1945, a B-29 bomber dropped a single atomic bomb on Hiroshima. Tens of thousands of Japanese were killed in less than a minute. Three days later, another such bomb fell on Nagasaki. On August 14, Japan surrendered to the United States and its allies. World War II, one of the most terrible wars in world history, was over.

The Marines had almost ninety-two thousand total casualties (killed and wounded) during World War II. This was a shockingly high number for the smallest branch of the major services. The Marines made up less than 5 percent of the Americans who fought in World War II, yet the Corps suffered 10 percent of the country's total casualties.[7] Unfortunately, this would not be the last action they would see in the twentieth century.

Four

Duty in War and Peace

Half my casualties were from [Vietnamese] guerrillas, and these were the nasty kind of casualties—the dirty war.[1]

> —General Lew Walt, who
> commanded Marine forces in
> Vietnam in the late 1960s

The Corps and the Changing World

More than one million Americans were killed or wounded in World War II. Despite these appalling numbers, the American public supported the war. The vast majority of Americans in the World War II years believed they were engaged in a noble cause to defeat a very evil enemy. Major wars the United States fought after 1945 lacked the sense of mission that prevailed in World War II. Conflicts in Korea and Vietnam were episodes of what was called the Cold War. Mostly a war of words, the

Cold War was a fifty-year-long struggle between the Communist and capitalistic systems. Often the two sides provided support for countries friendly to their system. In Korea, the communist governments in the Soviet Union and China gave aid to the North while the United States assisted South Korea. Americans, comfortable in their homes, felt little fear of Communist armies storming their towns and cities. The wars against terrorism that took place after September 11, 2001, stirred up passionate patriotic feelings. But some Americans questioned the Iraq War that began in 2003. After the war had gone on for months, it was generally believed that Iraq had little if anything to do with terrorist attacks on the United States. By 2005, more Americans had begun to question the war.

Marines fought in all post-World War II conflicts. As was true with civilians, some individual Marines puzzled over the wisdom of their country's involvement in certain wars. However, the men and women of the Corps kept their misgivings in their private thoughts. Duty is a tradition in the USMC. Marines obey orders.

Korea, the Forgotten War

On the morning of June 25, 1950, artillery roared over the 38th Parallel, the dividing line between Communist-ruled North Korea and South Korea. When the firing lifted, Soviet-built T-34 tanks led thousands of North Korean infantrymen into an attack on their southern neighbors. The Korean War had begun.

American troops were rushed to South Korea to stem the Communist advance. At first the American-led forces were pushed backward on the Korean Peninsula. Bravely, they defended a tiny corner of the land called the Pusan Perimeter. On September 15, 1950, army General Douglas MacArthur ordered soldiers and Marines to land at the port city of Inchon, which was far behind the Pusan front. For Marines, Inchon would be the last major ship-to-shore invasion they would make while under fire. Battling tricky tides as well as the enemy, the Marines established a beachhead at Inchon and marched inland. General MacArthur later wrote, "The Marines and Navy have never shone more brightly than this morning."[2]

The Inchon landings shattered the North Korean resistance. In late 1950, American forces drove deep inside North Korea. Then, just before Christmas, bugles sounded over the North Korean hills. Responding to the bugle calls, thousands of Chinese soldiers charged the Americans. The Chinese army had intervened and launched a new and ugly chapter of the Korean War.

The sudden Chinese attack left men of the 1st Marine Division trapped near the Chosin Reservoir. Temperatures fell to 20 degrees below zero, and blinding snow pelted the Marines. In the face of blasting winds, the men began a 78-mile trek to the port city of Hungnam. Everyone walked over the frozen roads. Only the wounded and dead rode trucks. One wounded Marine saw "Bodies strapped on the barrels of artillery, on the sides of trucks, across hoods, anywhere there was space. They were rigid. A wounded guy next to me froze to death the second night."[3]

For the next two-and-one-half years, Americans and their United Nations (UN) allies fought

▲ Marines in action in Korea, 1951

Communist troops in Korea. It became a war of hills, as battles were concentrated on dismal rises in the earth. Americans gave nicknames to these places— Pork Chop Hill, Old Baldy, Heartbreak Ridge.

As the Korean War continued, the American public coped with the frustrating situation by ignoring events in that far-flung land. News of the Korean War slipped from page one in the newspapers to page seven or eight. Some political leaders suggested Korea was a "police action," not a war. But Marines battling for the stark hills knew this looked like war, smelled like war, and hurt like war. A grim joke was told at the fighting fronts: "If this is a police action, why didn't they send cops?"

Remembering the Forgotten War

Even today the Korean conflict is mentioned with a few paragraphs in history books instead of a chapter. For that reason, Korea is often called the Forgotten War. But more than thirty-three thousand Americans died in Korea.[4] Loved ones at home felt the same tragic sense of loss as they do in any war. In July 1995, President Bill Clinton dedicated the Korean War Veterans Memorial on the National Mall in Washington, D.C. Looming high off the ground are nineteen larger-than-life infantrymen who march cautiously toward an American flag. Their faces bear the haunting expressions of men at war—confused, frightened, lonely. The monument stands as a powerful reminder of the Forgotten War.

Vietnam

No war since the Civil War divided the American public as did Vietnam. The Vietnam War began in the late 1950s when Communist North Vietnam clashed with the armies of South Vietnam. Many believed this was an Asian civil war that Americans should avoid. American presence began with small forces, but it soon escalated.

Once more, the Marines were first to fight. In March 1965, two battalions of Marines, about thirty-five hundred men, were sent to South Vietnam to protect the airbase at Da Nang. This was a dramatic change in U.S. policy. Previously, only advisors and other special troops had served in Vietnam. The Marines were the first regular ground forces sent to the country. Those men of the Corps had no idea they were the start of a war that would last seven frustrating and bloody years.

By 1968, some eighty-five thousand Marines, a quarter of the Corps' strength, were serving in Vietnam.[5] The Marines fought major battles at Khe Sanh and in the Hai Lang Forest. The twenty-five-day battle for the city of Hue remains a bitter chapter in Marine history. Marines were reluctant to use artillery in Hue City because it was crowded with civilians. Blasting the houses with artillery shells would cause terrible civilian casualties. So the men patrolled the city with rifles and fought the North Vietnamese and Vietcong street by street and

▲ Marines fight alongside South Vietnamese soldiers in a 1969
skirmish near Dak To, Vietnam.

house by house. More than one thousand Marines
were killed or wounded in the ordeal at Hue.[6]

In 1982, almost ten years after the war ended,
the Vietnam Veterans Memorial was dedicated in
Washington, D.C. The memorial consists of a black
granite wall containing the names of more than
fifty-eight thousand U.S. citizens killed in the conflict. It was designed to bind the emotional wounds
the country suffered, and it is sometimes called the
"wall of healing." In his book *Marine Pride*, Marine
Captain Scott Keller said,

> . . . there is a flag pole at [the wall's base
> containing] the seals of all the services:

Army, Navy, Marines, Air Force, and Coast Guard. Every day throughout the year, a detachment from Marine Barracks Eighth & I marches to the flag and polishes the Marine Corps Emblem. The other services have never touched theirs. There is, perhaps, a lesson here.[7]

Tragedy in Lebanon

The Marines are often deployed as "peace-keepers." In this capacity they attempt to stop civil wars and riots before they escalate and kill many innocent people. In September 1982, a Marine unit was sent to the Middle Eastern nation of Lebanon to help keep order in the face of civil strife. Marine units slept in a four-story concrete building near the Beirut, Lebanon, airport. Early on a Sunday morning, October 23, 1983, a truck crashed through the fence surrounding the building. The truck was driven by a suicide bomber. It rammed through the building's main door and into the lobby. In the bed of the truck were explosives equal to six tons of TNT. An incredible explosion

▲ This composite photo poster honors the Marines who died in the 1983 bombing in Beirut, Lebanon.

tore apart the building, killing 241 Americans, 220 of them Marines.[8] It was a horrendous act of terrorism committed against Marines who had entered Lebanon as peacekeepers.

The Persian Gulf War

In July 1990, the Iraq leader Saddam Hussein invaded his neighbor, the oil-rich country of Kuwait. Iraqi troops occupied Kuwait despite the demands of the U.N. and other international authorities for them to withdraw. President George H. W. Bush sent American forces to other countries in the region. The forces of other nations joined them, and soon the Persian Gulf War began.

A full Marine expeditionary force, including infantry, tanks, helicopters, and fighter planes, participated in the Gulf War. Qualification requirements for joining the Corps had risen in recent years and the Persian Gulf War men and women reflected the new standards. These were the brightest, best-educated Marines ever sent to battle. Whereas only half the Vietnam-era Marines were high school graduates, almost 100 percent of the Gulf War Leathernecks had their diplomas. Intense training prepared the Marines for the desert warfare ahead.

The Iraqi air force was quickly neutralized, and the skies belonged to the American-led forces. Marine fighter planes worked closely with ground troops to eliminate Iraqi artillery. Marine General

A Marine holds a gun on an Iraqi prisoner in Sabahiah, Kuwait, during the 1991 Persian Gulf War. The Marines were searching the town for snipers.

Mike Myatt said, "We convinced [the Iraqi artillery crews] it wasn't smart to man their artillery pieces because every time they did Marine air would come rolling in on them."[9]

On February 24, 1991, fast-moving columns of Marine tanks and armored troop carriers stormed into Iraqi positions. At the time, many Marine units were equipped with the aging M60 tank. This tank was considered inferior to the M1 Abrams tank used by the Army. No matter. Marine tankers performed brilliantly at the Burquan Oil Field during the largest tank battle of the Gulf War. In a heavy fog and amid smoke from dozens of oil fires, Marine tanks destroyed thirty-nine enemy vehicles.

The ground operations of the Persian Gulf War lasted only two full days. American servicemen and

Marine Casualties in Major Twentieth-century Wars

	Killed in Action	Wounded	Total Casualties
World War I	2,457	8,894	11,351
World War II	19,733	67,204	86,937
Korea	4,267	23,742	28,009
Vietnam	13,067	88,633	101,700
Persian Gulf	24	92	116[10]

women (all branches) suffered 370 killed. The Iraqi army may have lost up to one hundred thousand troops. Many thousands of Iraqi civilians—the true number will never be known—died under a rain of American bombs and missiles.

The Humanitarian Missions

Marines are not only first to fight, but they are also often the first Americans called upon to save lives on global missions. These missions are called MOOTWs, an acronym for Military Operations Other Than War. During the MOOTWs, men and women of the Corps are called upon to feed starving masses deprived of food due to civil strife. Marines also provide medical assistance when natural disasters such as earthquakes and tidal waves strike.

In December 1992, Marines landed on beaches in the African nation of Somalia. They were prepared to fight if necessary, but hoped to avoid gun battles. Somalia had been torn by civil war for years. Meanwhile, the people of the nation starved. The U.N. and other international agencies sent food, but it was looted by warring armies. The Marines were deployed as a police force. They protected food supplies and made sure food was properly distributed to hungry people. The Leathernecks accomplished their mission and hunger was eased in the troubled country. Fittingly, the Somalia MOOTW was called Operation Restore Hope.

Marines returned to Africa in June 1997, this time on a rescue mission to the country of Sierra Leone

A five-year-long civil war in Sierra Leone left thousands of people killed and wounded. A particularly brutal warring faction took over the country in 1997 and allowed its soldiers to loot stores and attack foreigners. The Marines took charge of this chaotic situation. Quickly, the Leathernecks evacuated foreigners, including a large group of Americans. Those rescued hailed the Marines as heroes.

In December 2004, a gigantic tidal wave, called a tsunami, washed over Pacific shores. The tsunami

▲ Lance Corporal Donald Gray helps make dinner for Sri Lankan victims of the 2004 tsunami.

was one of the greatest disasters in human history. The great wall of water killed hundreds of thousands of people and left millions homeless. Marines joined other international forces to give medical assistance to the injured and to help restore order. On the island nation of Sri Lanka, Marine bulldozers rolled off naval ships. Immediately, the machines began to clear roads from debris and allow emergency supplies to reach cut-off villages. Said Gunnery Sergeant Juan Quijada of the 15th Marine Expeditionary Unit: "We'll be doing road-clearing projects and possibly airlift missions. We'll be here as long as we're needed. I hope it provides some relief to the people." Certainly the Sri Lankan people appreciated the Marine efforts. Said one man: "The Americans are very helpful, not just to Sri Lanka but the world."[11]

Five

Organization and Current Operations

There are only two kinds of people that understand Marines: Marines and the enemy. Everyone else has a second-hand opinion.[1]

—Anonymous

Makeup of the Corps

The United States Marine Corps is by far the smallest branch of the four major military services. The Marines have about one hundred seventy-seven thousand men and women on active duty and about thirty-two thousand reserves. By contrast, the Army has four hundred eighty thousand active duty members. Many Marines believe they are an elite, a superior branch of the services. People in the Army, the Navy, and the Air Force sometimes accuse Marines of being boastful. But Marines say they are simply proud of their own outfit.

Members of the Corps can be stationed anywhere in the world. Marines stand guard at all U.S. embassies. Hawaii and Japan have large Marine contingents. About 65 percent of all Marines are assigned to the Corps' three infantry divisions. These infantry divisions make up the Fleet Marine Force (FMF). The divisions are strategically stationed around the world. The 1st Marine Division is headquartered at Camp Pendleton near Oceanside, California. The 2nd Division is at Camp Lejeune near Jacksonville, North Carolina. The 3rd Division is on Okinawa, Japan.

The Marine Motto

The Marine motto is almost sacred to members of the Corps: *Semper Fidelis*, Latin words for "Always Faithful." A shortened version of the motto is "Semper Fi." This is a common greeting or a way of saying farewell among Marines. Letters and e-mail sent by Marines often end with "Semper Fi."

Marines remain soldiers of the sea. Leathernecks still specialize in amphibious, ship-to-shore warfare. In this capacity, the Corps works closely with the Navy. Experts agree that waging amphibious war is the most difficult and dangerous of all large-scale military missions.

The Corps has its own air arm. Marine aviation units are divided into three air wings. Each air wing is attached to an infantry division. Marine pilots fly fighter planes similar to those used in the Navy. In combat, the fighter planes provide close support to ground troops. The Corps also maintains a large fleet of helicopters.

The Reserves

More than thirty-two thousand men and women serve in the Marine Reserves. They are divided into three

▲ Reserve Marines land their Combat Rubber Reconnaissance Craft in a training exercise in West Africa.

groups: the Ready Reserve, the Standby Reserve, and the Retired Reserve. Members of the Ready Reserve train one weekend a month and serve two weeks of full-time duty each year. Ready Reservists are the first to be called into active duty if the need arises. The Standby Reserve is made up of those who have already served on active duty. The Standby men and women do not have weekend training obligations, but they may also be ordered into duty in times of emergencies. Retired Reserves are those who have served twenty years or more in the Corps and are now collecting pensions. Even the Retired Reserve can be pressed into emergency duty.

Newspaper writers sometimes call the Ready Reservists "part-time Marines" or "weekend warriors." These names fail to do them justice. All members of the Ready Reserve know they can be called up in a few days notice and find themselves in a combat zone shortly after the call-up. About half of the American forces now deployed in Iraq (Army and Marines included) are reservists. In May 2005, four Marine Reservists were killed when their armored truck hit a land mine near Karabilah, Iraq. Can those four Marines, who made the ultimate sacrifice, properly be called weekend warriors?

A typical reserve unit is the helicopter squadron HMLA 773, nicknamed Task Force Red Dog. The Red Dogs, as they call themselves, are from Georgia and Louisiana. All are established in civilian life. One is a pilot for Federal Express and another is an FBI agent. The squadron, which consists of three hundred men and nine helicopters, was activated in 2004 and sent to Afghanistan. Certainly the men missed their families. But they were Marines and they joined in the hunt for the master terrorist Osama bin Laden.

For six months the Red Dogs served in Afghanistan. While supporting ground troops, they flew helicopters through snowstorms and through thick fog. Several times, helicopters from the Red Dog Squadron engaged in firefights with Afghan rebels on the

Toys for Tots

A well-known charity run by Marine reservists is the Christmastime Toys for Tots program. Beginning in 1947, reservists started collecting used toys and distributing them to needy children. Today, reserve units gather new toys in unopened boxes for distribution. Every Christmas season, some 7 million children benefit from the Marine Reserves' Toys for Tots drive.

ground. Finally, the squadron was allowed to go home. But there the Reservists received depressing news. The squadron's active duty assignment was extended twelve months, and they were due to return to Afghanistan.

The Top Marine

The Marines' highest-ranking officer is a four-star general called the Commandant of the Marine Corps. In 2005, the commandant was General Michael W. Hagee. General Hagee graduated from the U. S. Naval Academy in 1968. Hagee has commanded troops in many difficult operations. He received numerous awards including the Bronze Star with a combat "V" for action in Vietnam. The commandant is appointed by the president of the United States. He holds the office for four years. Hagee is the thirty-third Commandant of the Marine Corps. The first commandant was Samuel Nicholas who served from 1775 to 1781.

Several famous commandants have risen to almost legendary status in Marine lore. Archibald Henderson, the fifth commandant served from 1820 to 1859. No other

General Michael W. Hagee, commandant of the Marine Corps, talks to Marines at Camp Taqaddum in Iraq on December 13, 2004.

commandant had a longer tenure than Henderson. For that reason, Henderson is called "the old man of the Marine Corps." John Archer Lejeune, the thirteenth commandant, led the Corps from 1920 to 1929. Lejeune saw combat in World War I and later developed amphibious warfare doctrine that was used by the Corps in World War II. The huge base in North Carolina, Camp Lejeune, is named for this memorable commandant. Alexander Archer "Archie" Vandergrift, the eighteenth commandant, was top Marine from 1944 to 1947. Early in World War II, Vandergrift commanded the 1st Marine Division on the assault of Guadalcanal. For his staunch defense of that island in the face of repeated enemy attacks, Vandergrift won the Medal of Honor.

The President's Own

Stationed permanently in Washington is the Marine Band. Consisting of roughly 160 members, it is the most famous military band in the United States. It is called "The President's Own" because it performs at all ceremonies concerning the nation's chief executive. The band traces its history back to the administration of Thomas Jefferson.

Band members are technically Marine-enlisted men and women. However, band personnel receive no rifle training nor are they sent to Marine boot camp. Those chosen for the Marine Band are music majors selected from the nation's best colleges. Many hold doctorates and master's degrees in their specialties. They play with spirit and technical precision. Experts regard the President's Own Band as one of the greatest military bands in the world.

Easily the most famous Marine Band leader was John Philip Sousa, who presided over the group from 1880 to 1892. Sousa grew up in Washington and loved band music. As a young boy, he was tempted to run away and join a circus band. Instead, he took over the Marine Band and led it to world fame. Called the March King, Sousa composed some of the most stirring marches ever written: "Semper Fidelis," "The Washington Post," "El Capitan," and "The Stars and Stripes Forever." Sousa's music is still performed and loved all over the world. He always strove to perfect his organization. Sousa once wrote, "the Marine Band is the national band . . . as great among bands as America is among nations."[2]

▼ "The President's Own" performs on New Year's Day, 2004.

The official home of the Marine Band is the historic Marine Barracks on the corner of 8th and I Streets in Washington. Built in 1806, it is known as the "oldest post in the Corps." The barracks building also houses the Commandant's Own Drum and Bugle Corps. A popular show for tourists and Washingtonians alike is the Evening Parade. This parade is a seventy-five-minute performance played out on Friday evenings at 8:45 during the summer months. The parade features the Marine Band, the Marine Drum and Bugle Corps, and the Marine Corps Silent Drill Platoon.

Current Operations—Iraq

In March 2003, Marines and Army troops swept into Iraq, and the ground war for that country began. The United States was supported by troops from Great Britain, Poland, and Australia. President George W. Bush ordered the war primarily because intelligence reports claimed the Iraqis owned weapons of mass destruction (WMDs). The president feared the Iraqi dictator, Saddam Hussein, would use those weapons on the United States and its allies. The WMDs included chemical and biological devices that could kill millions.

The ground war was violent but short. In just three weeks, American forces stormed into Baghdad, the capital of Iraq. It seemed the war in that country was over. However, the Americans never found any evidence that Iraqi forces had the dreaded WMDs.

Later, the Bush administration admitted its prewar intelligence concerning the WMDs was flawed.

After the fall of Baghdad, a new war began. It was called an insurgency, or a war of occupation, depending on one's point of view. Die-hard supporters of Saddam Hussein and insurgents who had come from other Middle Eastern countries fought the Americans. Iraqi ethnic groups fought each other, and the Americans were often caught in the middle of their battles. Saddam Hussein himself was captured by soldiers on December 13, 2003, yet the war raged on. Thousands of Iraqi civilians have died because of the war.

As of December 2005, at least six hundred twenty-five Marines had been killed in Iraq. A Texan pushed a comrade out of danger before he was gunned down by Iraqi rifle fire. A nineteen-year-old from Nebraska was killed by a roadside bomb near Baghdad. A twenty-one-year-old Marine was the victim of a land mine. A Marine who was born in central Mexico met his death in an ambush. The Mexican-American Marine was given a full military funeral in the village where he was born, while hundreds of his one-time neighbors watched.

By the end of 2005, more than 2,170 Americans had died in Iraq. At home, many Americans had come to believe that the war in Iraq was a mistake from the beginning. Individual Marines, of course, have their own opinions of the war. But they are Marines. They obey orders in the spirit of their motto—Semper Fidelis.

Operation Iraqi Freedom

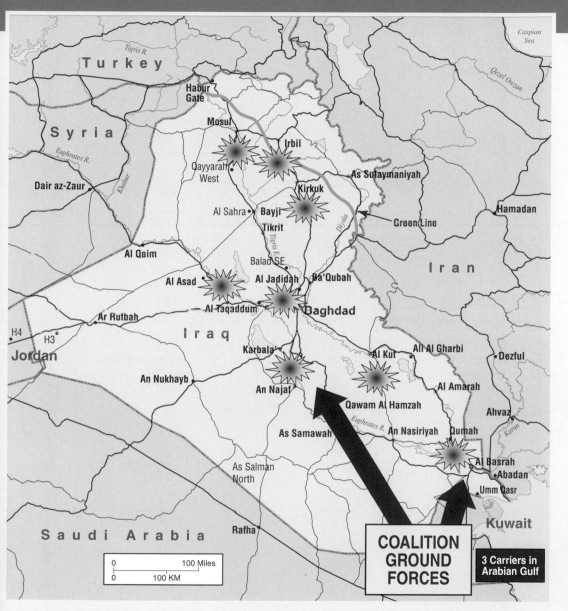

By March 25, 2003, coalition aircraft had already bombed many Iraqi positions ( ) and ground forces had started to advance into the country.

▲ A Marine stays down low on a battlefield in southern Iraq on March 23, 2003.

Six

The Making of a Marine

This is my rifle. There are many like it, but this one is mine.

My rifle is my best friend. It is my life. I must master it as I master my life.[1]

—The opening lines of "This Is My Rifle," which is recited by all Marine trainees. "This Is My Rifle" was written in 1942 by General William H. Rupertus.

Joining the Club

"So, you want to join the Corps? You want to sign up with MY Marine Corps? Are you good enough?" These are words typically used by Marine recruiters who greet young men and women entering their office. The recruiter certainly does not want to scare away an eager candidate. But the young person must know that only the best men and women are allowed to join the Corps and only the toughest can complete training.

In order to apply for enlistment, a person must be between eighteen and twenty-eight years of age. The Corps will reject anyone who has been convicted of a major crime. However, candidates who have had a minor brush with the law can be accepted. A high school diploma is not a requirement, but far more than 90 percent of Marine enlistees have completed high school. One must be in excellent physical condition to gain admission. Candidates cannot use drugs.

Think of the Corps as an exclusive club. The Marines set high standards for new club members to join. Many young applicants are rejected for various

Lance Corporal Crystal Dishong stands outside a Marine recruiting station.

The Youngest Recruits

A seventeen year old can join the Corps with his or her parents' written permission. Years ago, seventeen-year-old Marines were common, but these days they are a distinct minority. The official *Marine Corps Almanac* says that in 2005 only 480 Marines (0.30 percent of the entire enlisted ranks) were under eighteen. Here is an enlisted age distribution of the Corps' youngest members.

Age	Number	Percent of Enlisted Marines
18	9,239	5.82
19	17,569	11.07
20	20,497	12.92
21	21,232	13.38[2]

reasons. Some are turned down because they scored low on intelligence tests. Others fail to qualify for physical reasons. Despite the lofty qualification standards, the Marines usually fill their ranks with ample recruits. Many young people interested in the military want to join what they consider to be the best branch.

In order to keep its total numbers at roughly 177,000 men and women, the Marine Corps must sign up 3,270 recruits each month. In February 2005, the Corps failed to sign up its full monthly quota. This was the first such failure in more than ten years. Marine recruiters blame the Iraq War.

The war is unpopular with many segments of the public, including parents of military-age sons and daughters. Said a recruiting sergeant in Virginia: "This morning I had a mom laugh at me and hang up the phone."[3] The same sergeant visited a high school where a teacher screamed at him in the hallway. The teacher claimed it was military recruiters such as him who caused the death of her son in Iraq.

For many years the United States relied on the draft to fill its military ranks. In theory, the draft required all young men to serve at least some time in one of the military branches. The country never drafted women. There were many exceptions made in the actual practice of the draft. College students could delay their service duties and even avoid them altogether by simply staying in school. These exceptions led to the bitter charge that the draft system was unfair. Rich youngsters who could afford to remain in college escaped going to war while poor young men were routinely sent to the fighting fronts. The United States ended the draft in 1973. The country now has an all-volunteer military.

Through its history, the Marines have depended on volunteer enlistees. In World War II and to a lesser extent during Vietnam, the USMC drafted young men. However, the vast majority of Marines and ex-Marines are volunteers. Most consider it not a duty but an honor to serve in the Corps.

Fall In!

All right. You have been accepted into the Marine Corps. Congratulations! Now comes the hard part: a three-month training program called boot camp.

"Sir, yessir! Sir, the recruit's name is . . ."

"I can't HEAR you."

"Sir, yessir! Sir the recruit's name . . ."

You better get used to this sort of talk—shouted at the top of your lungs—if you want to survive Marine Corps boot camp. The aim of boot camp is to diminish your individuality and make you part of a unit. You do not even use the simple pronouns "I" or "me" because those words reflect individuality. Instead, you stand at stiff attention and yell, "Sir, the recruit does not know how to disassemble the M16A2 rifle, sir!" or, "Sir, the recruit will obey all orders, sir!" To further repress one's own wants and pleasures, male recruits are given a "buzz cut," a haircut down to the scalp. The buzz cut makes the young men look at least somewhat alike. Females are allowed to keep their hair, but it must be cut close and kept neat.

The Marine Corps maintains two boot camps, also called Marine Corps Recruit Depots (MCRDs). One MCRD is at San Diego, California, and it trains male recruits who enlist from homes west of

▲ Paul Nixon, a boot-camp drill sergeant, instructs a future Marine at Parris Island, South Carolina.

Talking Like A Marine

After a few weeks of boot camp, the recruit begins to speak a new language: Marine Talk. Many Marine terms come from the Navy—a floor is a "deck," a wall is a "bulkhead," and the bathroom is a "head." However, some expressions are purely Marine. Here are some widely used Marine expressions and terms:

field day—A day when everyone pitches in to give the barracks a vigorous scrubbing.

gung ho—Words used to describe Marine enthusiasm; the term comes from a 1943 movie.

scuttlebutt—Rumors; a scuttlebutt is also a drinking fountain, a place where rumors are discussed.

squared away—A particularly neat and tidy Marine is said to be "squared away."

ooooo-rah—This is a battle cry that Marines began using shortly after the Vietnam War. No one knows its origin, but it is similar to the Russian army's World War II battle cry: uuuuu-rah.

the Mississippi River. The other MCRD is at Parris Island, South Carolina, and it receives male recruits from states east of the Mississippi. All female recruits are sent to Parris Island regardless of where they live. Men and women recruits get almost the same training. During basic training, men and women are housed in separate barracks and work in separate units. In boot camp, there is little mixing of the sexes.

Which is tougher: the boot camp at Parris Island (PI) or the one at San Diego? Training routine at the two camps is identical. Yet the PI graduates claim their experience is more intense because they cope with the heat and the biting sand fleas in South Carolina. PI Marines call their San Diego counterparts "Hollywood Marines" for the base's California location. It is impossible to determine, really, which is the toughest boot camp. Still, the arguments between PI and San Diego have raged in Marine barracks for well more than fifty years.

Why these training bases are called boot camps is another legend of the Corps. One story says that in the old days, the first item issued to a recruit was a pair of boots. Therefore MCRDs were always called boot camps. Whatever the origin of the name, boot camp is a basic training facility. All branches of the service require basic training for new enlistees. But no other basic training program is tougher than Marine boot camp.

Life for a recruit centers around his or her platoon. The platoon has eighty members. Each platoon is run by four sergeants who are called drill instructors (DIs). The DI is a demanding boss, a parent figure, and a teacher all forged into one rock-hard Marine. Under the eyes of the DI, recruits learn to march with the M16 rifle. Recruits also disassemble their rifles, meticulously clean them, and memorize the proper names of each tiny part. In a few weeks, a recruit can take the rifle apart and put it back together again blindfolded.

The DI is also a physical education instructor and leads the platoon in vigorous exercise sessions. All recruits must pass a basic test that includes three

▲ Private Jeff D. Noel, Jr., does pull-ups during an afternoon physical training session.

pull-ups, forty sit-ups performed in two minutes, and a three-mile run completed in twenty-eight minutes. Not everyone can keep up with the rigorous program. A small number of men and women recruits are dismissed from the Corps for various reasons during the three months of boot camp. Perhaps the recruits cannot meet the physical demands of marching and vigorous exercise. Some recruits break down psychologically and are released from boot camp.

Food in boot camp is good and plentiful. One must eat properly in order to endure the physical demands of training. However, if a recruit is overweight, he or she is given a "diet tray" with low-fat and low-calorie foods. Those who are underweight are fed extra rations. Building strength and toughness is a boot camp goal.

Week six is devoted to weapons training. Recruits "snap in," meaning they practice various firing positions without actually discharging their rifles. Target shooting is next. Young Marines are given points and grades for the accuracy they achieve: 190 points earns a Marksman's badge, 210 a Sharpshooter, and 220 an Expert. Recruits are also taught to shoot either right-handed or left-handed and to fire their rifle while wearing a gas mask.

The ultimate physical challenge facing recruits comes in the final week with an ordeal called the Crucible. For fifty-four hours recruits endure live firing and close combat exercises. All these training duties require close cooperation between platoon members. In one cooperation drill, recruits deliberately fall backward into the waiting arms of their fellow platoon members. The men get only four hours of sleep and are fed limited rations. The Crucible is capped off with a brisk nine-mile hike with rifles and full packs. In San Diego, the hiking

▲ Marines crawl through the mud beneath barbed wire on the second day of the Crucible.

Enlisted Ranks, Salaries, and Pay Grades

Rank	Pay Grade	Approximate Salary*	Insignia
Private	E-1	under 4 months: $1,175 per month over 4 months: $1,270 per month	No insignia
Private First Class	E-2	$17,100 per year	
Lance Corporal	E-3	$18,000–20,400 per year**	
Corporal	E-4	$19,200–24,000 per year	
Sergeant	E-5	$21,600–30,000 per year	
Staff Sergeant	E-6	$24,000–36,000 per year	
Gunnery Sergeant	E-7	$27,600–49,200 per year	
Master Sergeant	E-8	$39,600–55,200 per year	
First Sergeant	E-8	$39,600–55,200 per year	
Master Gunnery Sergeant	E-9	$48,000–64,800 per year	
Sergeant Major	E-9	$48,000–64,800 per year	
Sergeant Major of the Marine Corps	E-9	$48,000–64,800 per year	

* Approximate salaries are as of 2006 and do not include food and housing allowances, free healthcare, money for college, and bonuses.
** Salary for ranks E-3 through E-9 depend on the number of years in service.

trail leads up a killer hill called, appropriately, the Grim Reaper.

Two rewards await the recruit finishing the Crucible: First, the recruit is served a "warrior's breakfast" consisting of steak, eggs, and pancakes. Second, the recruit receives the official Marine Corps Emblem—the globe and anchor—to wear on his or her collar. The emblem is a badge of honor.

Graduation from boot camp is marked with a full dress parade. Men and women graduates have paid in sweat, pain, and perhaps a few tears to take their place on this parade ground. As the band plays "The Marine Corps Hymn," the boot camp survivors know they are Marines now—and they will be for the rest of their lives.

Officers and Gentlemen

Young officers, signing up with the Corps, come from the nation's colleges and universities. Some future lieutenants are graduates of the U.S. Naval Academy at Annapolis, Maryland. Still other officers-to-be are recruited from the Corps' enlisted ranks.

Officers comprise about 10 percent of all Marine personnel.[4] For every eight enlisted men and women there is one officer. The other four military branches have a far greater percentage of officers in their ranks.[5] In the Marines, senior enlisted men (non-commissioned officers, called NCOs) assume a greater leadership role.

Officers do not go to boot camp. Instead, they attend Officer Candidate School (OCS) in Quantico,

Officer Ranks, Salaries, and Pay Grades

Rank	Pay Grade	Approximate Salary per Year*	Insignia
Second Lieutenant	O-1	$28,800–36,000	
First Lieutenant	O-2	$32,400–45,600	
Captain	O-3	$38,400–62,400	
Major	O-4	$43,200–73,200	
Lieutenant Colonel	O-5	$50,400–86,400	
Colonel	O-6	$61,200–105,600	
Brigadier General	O-7	$82,800–120,000	
Major General	O-8	$99,600–135,600	
Lieutenant General	O-9	$140,400–$150,000	
General	O-10	$160,800–$170,400	

*Salaries are as of 2006 and do not include food and housing allowances, free healthcare, money for college, and bonuses; also, an approximate salary range has been given for each rank.

Virginia. In many respects, OCS is as physically demanding as boot camp. The future lieutenants learn to march and fire weapons. The motto of OCS is *Ductus Exemplo* (leadership by example). This means the junior officers must be willing to do all the tasks and take all the risks expected of the enlisted men and women. Soon, graduates of OCS will lead a platoon in the field. Perhaps they will be in a combat situation shortly after their OCS experience. They are expected to set sound examples to command the respect of the enlisted ranks.

Warrant Officer Ranks, Salaries, and Pay Grades

Rank	Pay Grade	Approximate Salary per year*	Insignia
Warrant Officer	W-1	$28,300–45,300	
Chief Warrant Officer Two	W-2	$32,100–52,500	
Chief Warrant Officer Three	W-3	$36,500–60,400	
Chief Warrant Officer Four	W-4	$39,900–69,700	
Chief Warrant Officer Five	W-5	$68,600–75,700	

* Salaries are as of 2006 and do not include food and housing allowances, free healthcare, money for college, and bonuses; also, an approximate salary range has been given for each rank.

Gunnery Sergeant Eric Budde comes up for air while on the OCS's Staff Training Course.

OCS is a ten-week course. As is true with boot camp, the officer candidates march, study Marine Corps history and traditions, and fire weapons. At the end, the officers endure their own version of the Crucible. In a five-day program called "War Week," they work under simulated combat conditions while learning to lead men into battle. After OCS, officers attend the Basic School, six more months of intense physical training. All young lieutenants come to understand that a Marine officer is a leader who is entrusted with the lives of fellow Marines.

Seven

Being a Marine

Today's Marine forces continue to demonstrate the readiness, agility, and lethality the Nation demands from its armed forces in uncertain times.[1]
—General Michael W. Hagee, commandant of the Marine Corps, writing in 2005

Riflemen—First and Foremost

Regardless of their jobs or their assignments, all Marines are riflemen first. This policy—riflemen first—has been drummed into Marines for generations. Even officers destined to become fighter pilots in the air wing are taught basic infantry skills before their flight training begins. Young Marines learn the rifleman tradition immediately after boot camp.

Upon graduation from boot camp, a Marine is sent to the School of Infantry. This is a fifty-two-day course of intense combat training. The first fourteen days at the special school are devoted to what is called a Common Skills Package. Here a Marine learns how to detect and fire at targets in the field. Such field firing is a new concept as opposed to target shooting on the rifle range in boot camp. Also in the School of Infantry, Marines learn deadly tasks such as hand grenade throwing and disarming land mines.

The Automatic Rifle

All Marines must become familiar with the Squad Automatic Weapon (SAW). The SAW fires automatically like a machine gun. At 15 pounds the SAW is easily carried by one Marine. It uses either a 30-round magazine or a 200-round plastic package. Marines have employed such weapons since the days of the Browning Automatic Rifle (BAR), which was developed before World War II.

After completing the Combat Skills course, male Marines branch off to become specialists in infantry weapons. The men learn how to fire and maintain machine guns, mortars, and antitank guided missiles. Female Marines take the Combat Skills Package, but they do not train in special infantry weapons. By law, women are forbidden on fighting fronts during combat. Therefore, it is deemed unnecessary to teach female Marines special weapons skills.

Once they have completed the School of Infantry, most Marines will be assigned to one of the three infantry divisions. There they will need no reminder that the Marine's primary job is to carry a rifle into battle. The infantry divisions constantly train so they will be ready for combat assignments.

The M16, The Marine Rifle

Marines enter combat with the M16 rifle. Versions of the M16 have been employed by the Marine Corps for more than thirty years. At first the rifle was cursed because it frequently jammed up in the field and failed to fire. Through the years, the rifle has been refined and improved. It now functions very well under all conditions—from tropical jungles to the snows of northern lands. The rifle can be fired

▲ A Marine looks through the site of his M16A4 rifle while searching for insurgents in Iraq.

Force Recon

If Marines are the best infantry troops in the world (and they believe they are), a small group called Force Recon can be hailed as the best of the best. Force Recon is an outgrowth of the Marine reconnaissance companies that once scouted the terrain far ahead of advancing infantry units. Today, members of the Force Recon endure the most physically demanding training in the Marine Corps. Recon men practice parachute jumping as well as underwater diving. They are sent on grueling hikes. They learn to find their way over difficult terrain in day or night. All are volunteers.

semiautomatically (each trigger pull discharges one bullet) or it can be fired in bursts of three rounds. The M16A2 is 39.63 inches long and weights 8.79 pounds with a 30-round magazine.

Tools of War

The infantry would be at a serious disadvantage without supporting weapons such as artillery, tanks, and armored personnel carriers. The Fleet Marine Force relies on amphibious craft to get the infantry from ships to shores. Such highly technical vehicles and weapons require their own specialists to keep them in operation.

Artillery pieces propel high explosive shells long distances into enemy-held positions. The mainstay of Marine artillery is the 155mm howitzer. Most are towed weapons, meaning they are pulled by a truck. The latest version of the 155 is called the M777E1. This new edition of the 155 fires the same high explosive shell, but is six thousand pounds lighter than the old model. Loading and firing artillery pieces requires intense teamwork. A well-drilled squad moves with the precision of ballet dancers as they pass the rounds forward, make gun correction,

Marines prepare to fire a M777 lightweight Howitzer during a desert exercise.

and fire. Experienced crews on a 155 can shoot four shells a minute.

Today, Marines still specialize in ship-to-shore assaults. During World War II and Korea, that meant taking the slow-moving, lightly armored amtracs into battle. World War II men are shocked when they look at today's seagoing assault vehicles. Long ago, the Amphibious Assault Vehicle (AAV) replaced the World War II-era amtrac. Modern AAVs have armor plating, and they carry up to twenty-one combat-loaded Marines. On land the AAVs travel at twenty to thirty miles an hour. But the AAV moves only about six miles an hour in the water. The latest assault vehicle is the Landing Craft Air Cushion (LCAC). Riding on a cushion of air, the LCAC can carry a six-hundred-ton payload over the waves at the astonishing speed of almost fifty miles per hour. Air cushions, formed by huge propellers, allow the LCAC to skirt up a beach and give the Marines aboard a dry foot landing.

It is the Marines' job to land on hostile shores. It is the Navy's job to get them there. The Navy uses special amphibious assault ships to take Marines to their assigned beaches. The *Tarawa* and the *Wasp* are examples of assault ships used to transport Marines. The vessels resemble aircraft carriers. They are almost three football fields in length. Helicopters and light fighter planes take off from their flat decks. The Marines live below decks until they are called upon to board helicopters and landing craft for the assault. Thus, the ships allow Marines to approach enemy shores through the air or over the waves. Sometimes the ships that make up the amphibious assault fleet are called "Gater Freighters" and the fleet is known as the "Gater Navy."

Though Marines are a light infantry force, they use the nation's heaviest tank. Fully loaded, the M1A1 Main Battle Tank (used by the Army as well as the Marine Corps) weights 67.7 tons. It is armed with a powerful 120mm gun that is aimed with the aid of electronic devices. The accuracy of this gun is

▲ An LCAC is about to land on a beach during an exercise in Skiros, Greece.

amazing. It can hit a target more than 2.5 miles away. The M1A1 has a crew of four: a driver, a gunner, a loader, and the commander. It is hailed as the best tank in the world.

The primary light armored vehicle for the Marines is Light Armored Vehicle-25 (LAV-25). This is an armored personnel carrier propelled by eight wheels. The vehicle is sometimes called a "battle taxi" because it drives men to the fighting fronts. It has a crew of three and is capable of carrying six troops. Weighing twenty-four thousand pounds, the LAV-25 can reach sixty miles per hour on the ground. As an amphibious vehicle, it runs at about six miles per hour on the water. The LAV-25 is armed with a 25mm chain gun and a 7.62mm machine gun.

To defeat enemy tanks and armored personnel carriers, the Marines employ a lethal device called the Dragon. A shoulder-held weapon, the Dragon can be the Marine's best friend in combat. The tube-shaped device weighs forty-eight pounds. Ground troops simply aim the Dragon at enemy vehicles and fire. Its round has a special charge that enables it to penetrate thick armor. The Dragon can destroy a thirty-five-ton tank. An older antitank weapon called the TOW is also used by the Corps.

The Air Arm

Marine aircraft may be divided into three categories: fixed-wing, rotary wing, and—the newest model—tilt rotor. All three types operate from ships or from land.

Fixed-wing planes include swift fighters and dive bombers. The primary Marine fighter plane is the F/A-18D Hornet. This twin-jet aircraft clears enemy planes from the skies and provides ground support for Marine infantry. The Hornet is capable of reaching speeds up to 1,100 miles per hour. The plane has a 20mm cannon mounted in its nose and it can carry thirteen thousand pounds of bombs or missiles. Hornets can operate either from aircraft carriers or from advanced land bases.

Another fixed-wing aircraft used by the Corps is the AV-8B Harrier II. The Harrier is slow by jet standards (its maximum speed is about 660 miles per hour). However, the Harrier has a unique way of directing its jet exhaust downward. This downward thrust enables

CAREER PROFILE

John Glenn, First in Space

Easily the most famous Marine fighter pilot was John Glenn, who was born in Ohio in 1922. Glenn flew fighter planes for the Marines in World War II and in the Korean War. In 1959, he and six other men were chosen for the Mercury program.

The aim of the program was to put Americans in space. On February 20, 1962, Glenn blasted off in his tiny Mercury space capsule and circled the earth three times. His flight lasted less than five hours.

Glenn was the first American ever to orbit the earth. He became a national hero because at the time, most Americans believed the Soviet Union was far ahead of the United States in space exploration.

In 1974, Glenn was elected senator from Ohio. In 1998, at age seventy-seven, Glenn visited space again, becoming the oldest person to do so.

the plane to take off vertically like a helicopter. Short take-off and landing requirements make the

Harrier particularly useful in Marine ship-to-shore operations. The Harrier can also hover in the air, fly backwards, or fly in a tight circle.

Marines use two primary types of helicopters: those designed to attack ground targets and those made to transport troops or cargo. Helicopters are called rotary wing aircraft because their propellers are in fact wings that rotate.

The attack helicopter is basically a gunship. Attack helicopters fire on enemy ground troops with machine guns or with rockets. The latest Marine attack helicopter is the AH-1W Super Cobra. This helicopter carries a 20mm cannon with 750 rounds of ammunition. Manned by a crew of two officers, it is also armed with rockets and a wide variety of precision-guided missiles. Some missiles mounted on Cobras are designed to shoot down enemy helicopters. The Cobra is capable of reaching speeds of 160 miles per hour. In the 1991 Iraq War, Cobras destroyed almost one hundred Iraqi tanks.

Transport helicopters speed troops on various missions. In combat conditions, most transport helicopters will be armed with an auxiliary machine gun. An important Marine transport helicopter is the CH-46E Sea Knight. The Sea Knight has a crew of four and can carry fourteen combat-loaded marines. Its maximum speed is 160 miles per hour. The Sea Knight can be used to evacuate wounded Marines. In such cases, it becomes a first aid station in the sky. When doing medical evacuation work, the

▲ The AH-1W Super Cobra attack helicopter

Sea Knight can carry up to fifteen stretcher cases and two attendants.

A true workhorse as a cargo-carrying helicopter is the CH-53E Super Stallion. This mighty rotary winged aircraft has a crew of four. Almost seventy thousand pounds of equipment or cargo can be stuffed into the Super Stallion's huge interior.

An old favorite among Marine pilots is the UH-1N Huey Helicopter. A versatile craft, the Huey can be fitted for various missions. Versions of the Huey have served the Marines since the 1960s.

The Marines' latest troop-carrying aircraft is the MV-22 Osprey. It is a tilt rotor plane, combining the qualities of rotary wing and fixed-wing designs. The Osprey has two rotors mounted on a wing. For takeoffs, the rotors and wing are pointed upward. This allows the craft to rise like a helicopter. In the air, the wings and the rotors are shifted to the level position so the Osprey can fly like a fixed-wing airplane. The rotor and wing shift takes just twelve seconds to complete.

The advantages to the Osprey design are obvious. Carrying twenty-four infantrymen, the Osprey rises straight up. In level flight, it flies like an airplane. It is twice as fast and has twice the range of the average helicopter. The Osprey, however, is a new concept in aviation. As an entirely new type of craft, it has been plagued with problems. The airplane has crashed frequently, resulting in the deaths of more than thirty crew members and passengers. It is also a very expensive airplane, costing more than $24 million each.

Robot Spies in the Sky

The official Marine digest, *Concepts and Programs*, reads, "In Iraq, battles are won on intelligence first, bullets second."[2] Bearing that concept in mind, the Corps has developed several unmanned aerial vehicles (UAVs). These robotic aircraft serve as eyes in the air. Flying without a pilot, they relay television pictures of enemy movements back to ground commanders. Some UAVs are small and look much like model aircraft. The most up-to-date spy aircraft is called Eagle Eye. A tilt-wing UAV, the Eagle Eye penetrates far and high to spy on the enemy. Many UAVs are so small they do not appear on enemy radar. They can readily be sent into "hot spots" without risking the life of a pilot.

Vehicles for Support and Supply

Not all Marine vehicles are designed to operate directly on battlefronts. The Corps uses trucks and cars for the everyday tasks of hauling food to camps or carting garbage out of camps. These ordinary vehicles are not as exciting as frontline transports, but they play a vital role.

A vehicle seen in all units is the High Mobility Multipurpose Wheeled Vehicle (HMMWV), popularly called the Humvee. A rugged small truck, the Humvee can traverse over rough country where there are no roads. It can be fitted to play a variety of roles.

Humvees act as ambulances, antitank missile launchers, and troop carriers.

The Iraq War brought out a weakness in the Humvee. The light truck has no armor protection. Marines often patrol in hostile territory aboard Humvees. Patrols took terrible casualties when the vehicle struck a land mine or was hit by rocket propelled grenades. Clever Marine engineers welded scrap metal to the Humvee's sides to protect against grenade attacks. Later Humvees arriving in Iraq were equipped with armor protection.

The most common truck seen in the Corps is the seven-ton truck. These trucks transport troops, ammunition, and supplies. They also pull trailers and light artillery guns. Maximum payload for this vehicle is 30,000 pounds when traveling over

A Marine mans a TOW anti-tank missile system atop his Humvee while on patrol south of Kandahar, Afghanistan on December 7, 2001.

roads and 15,000 pounds when driving cross-country. They are not amphibious, meaning they cannot "swim" across water. But a special folding kit that extends the exhaust pipe and the air intake allows the truck to cross a river up to seven feet deep.

When he is in Washington, the Commandant of the Marine Corps rides in a civilian limousine painted in Marine green. Unique to the commandant's car is the license plate number—1775, the year the Marine Corps was born.

Marines employ a wide variety of specialized trucks and other vehicles. A huge truck called Container Transport Rear Body Unit can carry a payload of about 22.5 tons. Another heavy truck is the Recovery/Wrecker Body Unit. It is designed to tow damaged vehicles to repair shops. The wrecker is equipped with a derrick and can pull vehicles off the road in minutes. Smallest of the service vehicles is the KLR 250-D8 Marine Corps Motorcycle. Weighing 258 pounds, the motorcycle is used to speed maps and other documents from unit to unit.

Eight

The All-American Corps

The personal ties between a Marine and his Corps are strong. Marines believe in their Corps. They also believe that they are the best. They insist the "M" in "Marine" be capitalized. The highest accolade they can bestow on a member of another service is "He would make a good Marine."[1]

—Edward M. Simmons,
Marine Brigadier General (retired)
and historian, writing in 1997

The Marine Family

The Corps reflects the nation. It is made up of men and women of all races and nationalities. Since the Marines are a small service, its members think of themselves as a family. Typically, family members work together. Now and then, brother and sister Marines will argue among themselves. Still, all will help each other through the rough times of life.

As is true in the nation, the Marines thrive

in their diversity. America's strength comes from different racial and ethnic groups working together. Marines derive their strength from the same source. But this was not always the case. In the distant past, the Marine Corps was made up entirely of white males. Now the Marine family embraces all races and genders.

Women Marines

For years the Marines were reluctant to take women into their ranks. The first small unit of women Marines served in World War I and were used as clerks. After the First World War, women were banned from the Corps. During World War II, women reentered the Marines. The women joined the ranks despite the misgivings of older officers and enlisted men. A story was told that when the wartime Marine Corps announced it would take women recruits, a strange event took place. Immediately after the announcement, a portrait of the legendary Commandant Archibald Henderson fell off the wall at Marine headquarters in Washington. Of course, this portrait calamity is only a story.

Some nineteen thousand women Marines served in World War II.[2] They did not see action on combat fronts during the war. But those who thought the Corps was no place for females were proven wrong. Women Marines became cryptologists, puzzling out the enemy's decoded messages. Some were typists

Corporal Anne Hedrington uses a metal detector on a voter in Husaybah, Iraq, on December 15, 2005.

and stenographers. Still other World War II women Marines worked as truck mechanics.

Today, women make up about 6 percent of the total Marine force. This 6 percent figure is far lower than that achieved by other service branches. Experts believe young women are less attracted to the Marine Corps because they see fewer opportunities in the USMC. By law, women are not allowed in ground combat zones as part of infantry, tank, or artillery organizations. Most Marine units are geared for ground combat, and therefore cannot fully include women.

In many modern conflicts, the policy of keeping women away from combat zones is difficult to enforce. The war in Iraq is a guerrilla war. It has no clearly defined battle lines. Everyone stationed anywhere in Iraq can be killed or wounded by a car bomb or by an enemy rocket or grenade. Women Marines in Iraq do not serve side by side with men on combat patrols. However, the women still face grave dangers even if they work at a field hospital or direct civilian traffic.

The top woman Marine in Corps history is Carol Mutter. She joined the Marines in 1968, right after graduating from college. An expert in computers and mathematics,

Women in the Armed Forces

The distribution of women in the four major services as of 2003 stands as follows:

Service	Percent of Women
Air Force	19.60
Army	15.20
Navy	14.50
Marines	6.03[3]

Mutter was in charge of many highly technical projects. In 1996, she was promoted to lieutenant general. This gave Mutter three stars, ranking her as the only three-star female officer in the United States military. General Mutter retired from the Marines in 1999, after thirty-two years of service.

Racial Minorities

A regulation written in 1798 said, "No Negro, mulatto, or Indian" may join the Marine Corps.[4] Throughout its early history, membership in the USMC was restricted to whites only. Latinos and American Indians were allowed to join before World War II. African Americans were admitted into the Corps in 1942, but they were put in segregated units. In 1947, President Harry Truman signed an order forbidding segregation in all branches of the armed forces. The Marines were slow to integrate their ranks. However, by the early 1950s, blacks, whites, Hispanics, and other ethnic groups served together as equals in all units.

Racial Makeup of the USMC

According to the official *Marine Corps Almanac*, the racial figures of the 2005 Marine Corps stood as follows:

Officers	
White	15,392 (80 percent of the officer force)
Black	1,302 (14 percent)
Hispanic	1,116 (5 percent)
Other	1,029 (1 percent)
Total	18,839
Enlisted	
White	99,998 (63 percent of the enlisted ranks)
Hispanic	21,916 (14 percent)
Black	20,442 (13 percent)
Other	16,285 (10 percent)
Total	158,641[5]

In the segregated Marine Corps of World War II, a legendary Marine named Gilbert H. Johnson rose to prominence. Johnson had served in the Army. When he came to the Marine Corps in 1942, he was promoted to field sergeant major and was put in charge of all African-American drill instructors. Johnson made certain that African-American members of the Corps had the best basic training the services could provide.

Frank E. Petersen entered the Corps in October 1952 and became one of a handful of African-American Marine pilots. Petersen flew combat missions in the Korean War and in Vietnam. In 1979,

▲ Sergeant Major of the Marine Corps John Estrada addresses Marines in Kunar Province, Afghanistan, in December 2004.

Frank Petersen was the first African-American Marine to be promoted to general.

While the commandant is the top Marine officer, the Corps also reveres its senior-enlisted man. In 2005, that honor went to John L. Estrada. As the highest-ranking enlisted man, Estrada has the title sergeant major of the Marine Corps. Sergeant Estrada enlisted in September 1973 and served in many capacities including as a drill instructor in Marine Boot Camp. On June 26, 2003, he was the sixteenth person granted the title sergeant major of the Marine Corps.

Marine Lieutenant Billy Mills is a Sioux Indian who was born on the Pine Ridge Reservation in 1938. Lieutenant Mills was an outstanding Marine officer. He was also an outstanding long-distance runner. In 1964, he went to the Olympic Games in Tokyo, Japan, to compete in the 10,000-meter run (a little over eight miles). No one gave the Marine lieutenant a chance to win. Americans at the time simply were not distance runners. The 10,000-meter race had never been won by an American athlete. Sioux

▲ Billy Mills shoots a starting pistol to begin the Marine Corps Marathon on November 4, 2004.

pride and Marine pride motivated Lieutenant Billy Mills. He shocked the experts by winning the race and bringing home the Olympic gold medal. In 1983, a movie called *Running Brave* was made to celebrate his achievement.

The Marine Corps' Policy on Homosexuals

The Marine Corps follows a policy of "don't ask, don't tell" with homosexual members. This means that if one is gay, he or she is not supposed to say so to other Marines. Conversely, no one is allowed to ask a Marine about his or her sexual orientation. It is a compromise measure. Since 1993, "don't ask, don't tell" has been the standard practice in all branches of the armed forces.

Living and Learning in the Marine Family

A Marine is never finished with school. Boot camp can be thought of as grade school. The fifty-two-day School of Infantry is the Marine equivalent of high school. Beyond that, Marines are likely to be assigned to one of dozens of schools to learn specialized skills. Even men and women who have been in the Corps for more than fifteen years can look forward to being reschooled. The life of a Marine is one of study and change.

The basic Marine Expeditionary Unit (MEU) is a self-contained force. The typical MEU has fifteen hundred to three thousand Marines. These men and women are always prepared to board ships and go to any trouble spot in the world on short notice. MEU's have their own air arm, their own artillery, their own trucks and other support vehicles. The unit requires the services of radio operators, mechanics, cooks and bakers, as well as ground-pounding infantry. Special skills require special training. The Marine's job is to learn.

A Marine must always keep his or her seabag packed. A seabag is the tubular traveling "suitcase" where Marines put all their gear. Marines are always on the move, and most members like it that way. The Marine Corps can be considered the nation's overseas police force. Wherever there is an emergency in the world, the call will sound—"send in the Marines." And of course the Marines will always respond.

Navy Corpsmen, Heroes of the Corps

One job a Marine cannot hold is that of a medic. Marines do not directly tend to wounded on the battlefield. Navy medics, called Corpsmen, are assigned to the Marine Corps to provide first aid and assistance to the wounded and the sick. Over the years, the Corpsmen have become heroes to the Marines. Particularly in World War II, Corpsmen exposed themselves to enemy fire in order to treat Marines. Between 1914 and 1969, twenty-one Navy Medical Corpsmen have won the Medal of Honor while serving with the Marines.

Abiding by Family Rules

The author of this book served three years in the Marines during the late 1950s. I remember a gunnery sergeant telling me, "It's easy to stay out of trouble in the Marines. Just fall in for all your formations and do what you're told. Easy!" The gunnery sergeant might have overemphasized the "easy" part, but his basic instruction was sound. Falling into formation means just that. When your company is called upon to "fall in" on the company street, you are expected to be there bright and alert. If you work in an office, "falling in" means you must be at your desk at the exact time you are ordered to report.

Looking like a Marine is always important. A Marine stands straight, no slouching. Hat is properly on one's head. Hands are not in one's pockets. Many Marines refuse to smoke or chew gum in public because they believe such practices bring disgrace to their uniforms.

The NCOs

More than any other branch of service the Marine Corps relies on its NCOs (non-commissioned officers) for leadership. An NCO is an enlisted leader and holds a status just below that of a commissioned officer (CO). All men and women, corporal and above, are NCOs. Upon becoming an NCO, he or she studies the Non-commissioned Officer's Creed:

> I am the backbone of the United States Marine Corps, I am a Marine Noncommissioned Officer . . . I will demand of myself all the energy, knowledge, and skills I possess, so I can instill confidence in those I teach. I will constantly strive to perfect my own skills and to become a good leader.[6]

It is a good idea to seek the advice and counsel of the senior men or senior women NCOs in your unit. Often this will be the gunnery sergeant or

▲ Marines and their drill instructor (left) fall in and report to the regimental drill master.

"Gunny." The gunnery sergeant is a concept unique to the Marines. He or she is a technical sergeant and is usually the highest-ranking enlisted man within a platoon of forty to sixty Marines. The gunnery sergeant is a sort of father figure for young Marines. The gunny can be a stern father. But leading a platoon is an enormous responsibility. Gunnies know the younger men and women yearn for fair guidance.

Nine

Risks and Rewards of Being a Marine

We are mad, not only individually, but nationally. We check manslaughter and isolated murders; but what of war and the much vaunted crime of slaughtering whole peoples?[1]

> —Seneca, the Roman philosopher who died in 65 A.D. In his writings Seneca often criticized his nation's leaders who let passion overtake their reason and bring Rome to war.

Rewards

President Ronald Reagan once said, "Some people spend an entire lifetime wondering if they made a difference. The Marines don't have that problem."[2] Just to successfully serve in the Corps is the reward of a lifetime. The Marines are a special group as every man and woman member of the group knows. Other military services admire the Marines, though they often do this reluctantly. All realize the

Marines have the toughest standards of admission, the toughest training, and they are given the toughest assignments.

Aside from the element of pride, service with the Marines is a job that offers pay and full benefits. The pay aspect is one few young Marines facing boot camp have time to think about. However, as a Marine, a man or woman is guaranteed food and lodging and complete health benefits. As long as one performs one's duties, there is no threat of layoffs. In times of an uncertain economy and a poor job market, military service beckons many high school grads. Do not expect to get rich. A beginning private entering boot camp has a military pay grade of E-1. This means the private earns $1,104 a month. Many civilian jobs open to high school grads pay three times that amount.

Marine pride stays with a person long after one's discharge. Marines who served together fifty or more years in the past get together to celebrate spirited reunions. The Marine experience is

Medals and Awards

On their dress uniforms, Marines proudly wear medals they were given for excellent performance of their duties. Not all medals are presented for bravery in combat. Here are some of the medals Marines are awarded:

Bronze Star—Given for exceptional performance in military operations.

Distinguished Service Medal—Presented only to officers who perform their duties with excellence.

Medal of Honor—The highest award given by the American military.

Navy Cross—Given to Navy personnel and Marines for exceptional gallantry in combat.

Purple Heart—Presented to those wounded or killed in combat.

Silver Star—Awarded for bravery beyond one's duty.

something a person will talk about and think about for a lifetime. In fact, many older veterans of the Corps refuse to say they are *ex*-Marines. They claim the prefix "ex" distances them from the USMC. They are Marines for life. So they call themselves "former" Marines rather than ex.

One former Marine was Ted Williams, who died in July 2002. In the 1940s and 1950s, Williams was one of the country's greatest baseball players. In his career, he hit 521 home runs. He was also a Marine officer and a pilot in World War II and in the Korean conflict. Williams maintained his experience as a Marine overshadowed his illustrious career as a ballplayer. He once said, "It's a funny thing, but as years go by, I think you appreciate more and more what a great thing it was to be a United States Marine. . . . I am a U.S. Marine and I'll be one till I die."[3]

▲ Captain Joshua L. Glover receives a silver star for leading his platoon to two victories in Fallujah, Iraq, on April 13, 2004.

Making the Corps a Career

Most men and women will serve a three- or four-year "hitch" in the Corps and then return to civilian life. They will find their Marine training to be invaluable in the years ahead. Infantry training, which all Marines go through, gives a person discipline and a sense of responsibility. Special skills such as mechanics or truck driving will apply directly to civilian jobs.

Many men and women will decide to forego civilian life and choose to remain in the Corps. Their ultimate goal is to establish a career and serve the Marines for twenty years before retiring. After twenty years as a Marine, a person will receive a generous pension and still be relatively young.

As their initial hitch or enlistment period expires, the Corps encourages its men and women to "ship over," or reenlist. Certainly it benefits the Marine Corps to keep experienced men and women in its ranks. When one "ships over," he or she receives a substantial cash bonus. Reenlisting Marines usually sign up for three or six additional years. Often, upon shipping over, a Marine will get his or her choice of duty assignments.

Embassy duty is one of the most prestigious

Famous People Who Were Marines

Actors and TV Personalities
- Gene Hackman
- Lee Marvin
- Ed McMahon
- Steve McQueen
- Burt Reynolds
- Montel Williams

Athletes
- Billy Mills (track star)
- Ken Norton (boxer)
- Leon Spinks, Jr. (boxer)
- Lee Trevino (golfer)
- Ted Williams (baseball star)

Business and Political Leaders
- James Baker (secretary of state)
- F. Lee Bailey (lawyer)
- John Glenn (U.S. senator from Ohio)
- John Murtha (U.S. representative from Pennsylvania)
- James Webb (secretary of the Navy)

jobs in the Marine Corps. A Marine contingent stands guard at every American Embassy building in the world. One has to reenlist to qualify for the special Embassy positions. Of course, even Embassy duty has its hazards. In November 1979 militant students stormed the American Embassy

▲ A Marine stands watch at the American embassy in India.

in Tehran, Iran, and held fifty-three Americans there captive. Among the hostages were thirteen Marines of the guard unit. The Marine guards had been ordered not to fire on the invading students. The Americans were held 444 days until their final release. One captive, muscular Marine Sergeant Rodney Sickman, frustrated his guards. Sickman challenged the Iranians to arm wrestling contests and beat them in every encounter.

Many interesting jobs and assignments are open to career Marines. More than 180 specialized skills are taught in Marine schools. Men and women learn electronics, weather forecasting, office management, construction, and dozens of other trades. But never forget, Marines are riflemen first. Anytime during the course of a career, one can expect a transfer to a combat unit.

The Fog of War

Making war is the ultimate task of the Marine Corps. All Marines prepare for war even though they hope they will never be called upon to fight. War is the most brutal, the most hurtful, the most danger-ous activity engaged in by humankind. Yet warfare will touch the lives of many Marines.

Traditionally, the Leathernecks are given tough and dangerous combat assignments. Consequently, they experience a severe rate of casualties. Also, the Marines tend to be younger than men and women of other services. Many Marines killed in battle

Two Notable Books Written about the Marine Corps by Marines at War

With the Old Breed at Peleliu and Okinawa by Eugene Sledge, is one of the most powerful of all World War II memoirs. As a young Marine, Sledge saw intense combat in the Pacific. His book is not always complimentary to his fellow Marines. In painful detail, Sledge describes how war can transform otherwise respectable young men and turn them into cruel, unfeeling brutes.

Tom Brady went to Korea as a Marine Lieutenant in 1951. In his book *The Marines of Autumn*, he describes how he and his men faced two enemies: the bitter cold as well as the Chinese and North Korean Communists. Brady's book is a novel and an absorbing account of a winter campaign during the Korean War.

are teenagers or men and women in their early twenties.

At the end of 2005, the United States had been at war in Iraq for more than two years. Young Americans sent to Iraq grew up watching war movies. Hollywood has a way of glamorizing warfare. Movies, especially those dating back to World War II, show fighting men heroically charging the enemy. The men charge as if they were unafraid of death. But this type of fearlessness is never the case in actual combat. The heat of battle can cause brave men and women to become almost frozen with terror. Certainly Marines and soldiers found fear, not Hollywood-style glamour, in the Iraq conflict.

In 100-degree heat, American forces patrol the dusty streets of Iraqi towns. Despite the suffocating heat, they are forced to wear heavy helmets and

A Marine says good-bye to his wife and baby before he leaves for Iraq. This will be his third deployment to the country.

body-protecting vests. A sniper's bullet or a hidden bomb might await them at any corner. Americans are seen by some Iraqis as foreign occupiers. Throughout history, people have hated occupying armies. Thus, the soldiers and Marines are targets for those willing to sacrifice their lives to drive them out of Iraq.

In early 2005, the 3rd Battalion, 2nd Marine Regiment, was ordered to put down rebels in the Iraq province of Al Anbar. This is one of the largest and most remote sections in Iraq. Dutifully, Marine tanks and truck columns moved into Al Anbar, which sprawled over thirty thousand square miles of desert wasteland. Any ditch or pothole along the road could hide a land mine. A parked car, a passing car, or a garbage can might contain a bomb.

Terror prevails in every war. Combat veterans agree that a man who says he is not afraid in battle is either a liar or a fool. The fear in war is constant and mind numbing. In Iraq, there are no routine patrols or easy assignments. In December 2005, ten Marines were killed when a hidden bomb blew up on the outskirts of the city of Fallujah. The Marines were on patrol in an area that many high-ranking officers thought to be secure.

Combat wounds are particularly horrible. Wounds in Iraq include legs blown off due to land mine blasts. In any war a soldier can lose a limb. In such cases, the screams of a wounded person can be heard blocks away. Other combat injuries result in agonizing burns and hideous facial scars. Thanks to

▲ A helmet on a rifle stands in honor of Lance Corporal Miguel Terrazas during a memorial service. Terrazas was killed by an improvised explosive device (IED) in Iraq.

the prompt medical assistance available today, few of those injured in Iraq die from their wounds. The survival rate among the Iraq wounded is far greater than in any previous war.

The stress of battle can leave scars beyond evident wounds to the body. The mind can endure only so much intense danger, only so many close brushes with death. Even after one leaves a combat zone, memories of combat danger can torment a person's inner thoughts. Veterans of any war can suffer from what is called post-traumatic stress disorder (PTSD). This condition was called "shell shock" in World War I and "combat fatigue" in World War II. It is a mental disorder brought about by the stress of war. Nightmares, an inability to concentrate, irritability, and alarming flashbacks to scenes of combat haunt a victim of PTSD. Such mental demons can plague a person for years.

In 1880, the American Civil War General William T. Sherman spoke to an audience. To those youths in the audience who dreamed about finding glory in war, the general said, "There is many a boy here today who looks on war as all glory, but, boys it is all hell."[4]

Anyone wishing to join the Marines must weigh the risks against the rewards. The Marine experience can be immensely rewarding for a young person—as it was for the author of this book. However, it must be remembered that the ultimate task for a Marine is to wage war. And war, as General Sherman once said, is all hell.

The Marine Corps of the Future

On November 10, 2005, the Marine Corps celebrated its 230th birthday. Through all its years, the Corps had been first to fight. The Marines remain a force in readiness. Their duties extend beyond waging war.

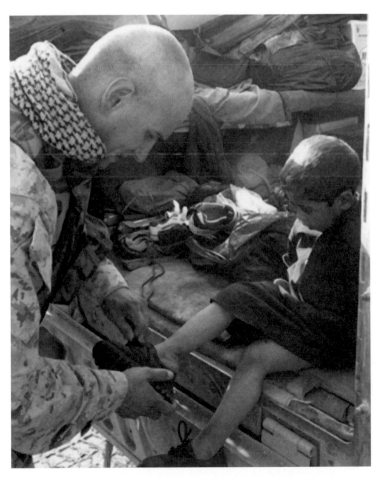

▲ A Marine puts new shoes on an Iraqi child as part of a humanitarian mission.

They enter the twenty-first century prepared to meet complex missions. In their new role, Marines are warriors as well as humanitarians and peacekeepers.

In 1998, the Commandant of the Marine Corps was General Charles C. Krulak. General Krulak looked to the future and wrote,

> In the twenty-first century our Marines will fight something we call the "three block war." In the morning they may be feeding and clothing displaced refugees—providing humanitarian assistance. A few hours later, they may be holding two warring factions apart—conducting peacekeeping operations. Later that night, they could be engaged in a lethal high-intensity urban battle. . . . To do this they must be as physically tough and as mentally agile as any who have borne the title U.S. Marine. And they will be!"
> Semper Fi.[5]

Author's Note

This picture was taken in 1956 on Okinawa when I served with Weapons Co., 3rd Battalion, 9th regiment, 3rd Marine Division. Our old outfit still gets together for very fun-filled reunions and we remain close friends despite the passage of some fifty years. The Marines pictured below are: (left to right) Sergeant Stearnes, Corporal Smith, Private Stein (the author), and Private Shoppell.

Timeline

November 10, 1775—The United States Marine Corps is created by an act of the Second Continental Congress; the official birthday of the Corps is still celebrated on November 10.

1776—During the American War of Independence, the U.S. ship *Alfred* lands 268 Marines on the British-held island of New Providence in the Bahamas; it was the Marines first amphibious operation.

1805—The Marines attacked pirate bases at Derna, Tripoli.

1814—In a War of 1812 action, a unit of Marines and sailors put up a spirited defense against British troops near Washington, D.C.

1847—During the Mexican-American War the Marines conquered palace grounds once used by the Aztec leader Montezuma.

1859—Marines led by Army Colonel Robert E. Lee capture the antislavery zealot John Brown at Harpers Ferry, Virginia (now West Virginia); John Brown's raid at Harpers Ferry was a major cause of the Civil War (1861–1865).

1898—In the Spanish-American War the Marines were the first troops to land in Cuba and the first to land in the Philippines.

1912—Marines land at Nicaragua to put down a revolution in that nation; the Nicaragua operation was an example of the "little war" the

1776

1805

1912

Marines have been called upon to fight throughout their history.

1917—Marines are transported to France to take part in World War I.

1918—The Marines fight the biggest battle thus far in their history at Belleau Wood in France.

1918—The first women join the Marines Corps; the first Marine airwing is established.

1926—The Marines again land at Nicaragua.

1941—The Japanese bomb Pearl Harbor on December 7, plunging the United States into World War II.

1942—Marines land at Guadalcanal to begin the U.S. World War II offensive in the Pacific.

1943—The four-day battle of Tarawa Atoll cost the Marines more than one thousand lives.

1944—Marines assault Peleliu, a dismal Pacific Island, and begin a bloody battle that lasts more than five weeks.

1945—In a terrible battle the Marines conquer Iwo Jima from Japanese defenders.

1945—Marines participate in the Battle of Okinawa, the costliest single battle in the Pacific War.

1945—World War II ends with Marine casualties listed as 19,733 killed and 67,204 wounded in almost four years of warfare.

1917–1918

1943

1945

1950—North Korea invades South Korea, thereby launching the Korean War.

1950–51—During a bitter winter campaign, surrounded Marines fight out of the Chosen Reservoir in Korea.

1953—The Korean War ends; the Marines have suffered 28,011 casualties in three years of fighting.

1950–1953

1962—Marine officer and pilot John Glenn becomes the first American to orbit the earth when his spacecraft, *Friendship 7*, blasted into the sky and circled the earth three times on February 20.

1965—Marines begin operations in Vietnam; they are the first regular troops the U.S. deployed in that country.

1968—In an assault on the Vietnamese city of Hue, the Marines suffer one thousand men killed or wounded.

1965–1973

1973—The Vietnam War ends; almost eight hundred thousand Marines have served in Vietnam over the years and more than thirteen thousand were killed during the fighting.

1983—A bomb planted by a suicide bomber kills 220 Marines in Lebanon.

1991—Marines take part in the Persian Gulf War.

1992—Marines serve as peacekeepers and help quell a civil war in the African nation of Somalia.

1991

1997—Marines return to Africa and help feed starving people in the war-torn nation of Sierra Leon.

2001—Marines are the first regular troops employed in Afghanistan after the September 11 terrorist attacks.

2003—Marines are key participants in the Iraq War.

2001

2004—Marines participate in humanitarian operations in various Asian countries after the December tsunami tidal wave took many thousands of lives and left millions homeless.

Chapter Notes

Chapter One   *First to Fight*

1. Associated Press release, June 26, 2004.
2. S. F. Tomajczyk, *To Be a U.S. Marine* (St Paul, Minn.: Zenith Press, 2004), p. 81.

Chapter Two   *The Few, the Proud: the Marines*

1. B.L. Crumley, *The Marine Corps* (San Diego, Calif.: Thunder Bay Press, 2002), p. 9.
2. Scott Keller, *Marine Pride* (New York: Kensington Publishers, 2004), p. 117.
3. Joseph H. Alexander, *The Battle History of the U.S. Marines* (New York: Harper Collins, 1999), p. 47.

Chapter Three   *Hell in the Pacific*

1. George Feifer, *The Battle of Okinawa* (Guilderford, Conn.: Globe Press, 2001), p. 258.
2. Rafael Steinberg, *Island Fighting* (Alexandria, Va.: Time-Life Book, 1978), pp. 112–113.
3. Ibid., p. 118.
4. Ibid.
5. E.B. Sledge, *With the Old Breed on Peleliu and Okinawa* (New York: Oxford University Press, 1981), p. 125.
6. Scott Keller, *Marine Pride* (New York: Kensington Publishers, 2004), p. 136.
7. Joseph H. Alexander, *The Battle History of the U.S. Marines* (New York: Harper Collins, 1999), p. 248.

Chapter Four   *Duty in War and Peace*

1. Joseph H. Alexander, *The Battle History of the U.S. Marines* (New York: Harper Collins, 1999), p. 352.
2. Ibid., p. 270.
3. Ibid., p. 291.

4. Harry G. Summers, *Korean War Almanac* (New York: Facts on File, 1990), p. 75.

5. Alexander, p. 360.

6. Ibid., p. 340.

7. Scott Keller, *Marine Pride* (New York: Kensington Publishers, 2004), p. 151.

8. Edwin Howard Simmons, ed., *The Marines* (Quantico, Va.: Marine Corps Heritage Foundation, 1998), p. 105.

9. Alexander, p. 376.

10. Albert A. Nofi, *The Marine Corps Book of Lists* (New York: Da Capo Press, 2000), pp. 39–40.

11. The Associated Press, "Marines Hit the Ravaged Beaches," *The Orange County Register*, January 11, 2005, <http://www.ocregister.com/ocr/2005/01/11/sections/nation_world/asia_pacificrim/Article_373053.php> (August 25, 2006).

Chapter Five *Organization and Current Operations*

1. S. F. Tomajczyk, *To Be a U.S. Marine* (St Paul, Minn.: Zenith Press, 2004), p. 135.

2. Edwin Howard Simmons, ed., *The Marines* (Quantico, Va.: Marine Corps Heritage Foundation, 1998), p. 241.

Chapter Six *The Making of a Marine*

1. S. F. Tomajczyk, *To Be a U.S. Marine* (St Paul, Minn.: Zenith Press, 2004), p. 47.

2. *Concepts and Programs* 2005 (an official U.S. Marine publication), p. 237.

3. *Chicago Tribune*, January 4, 2005, p. 1.

4. Tomajczyk, p. 64.

5. Ibid.

Chapter Seven *Being a Marine*

1. *Concepts and Programs* 2005 (an official U.S. Marine publication), opening page.

2. Ibid., p. 65.

Chapter Eight   *The All-American Corps*

1. Joseph H. Alexander, *The Battle History of the U.S. Marines* (New York: Harper Collins, 1999), p. xi.
2. Ibid., p. 248.
3. William A. McGeveran, ed., *The 2005 World Almanac and Book of Facts* (New York: World Almanack Education Group, Inc., 2005), p. 223.
4. Edwin Howard Simmons, ed., *The Marines* (Quantico, Va.: Marine Corps Heritage Foundation, 1998), p. 71.
5. *Concepts and Programs* 2005 (an official U.S. Marine publication), pp. 236–240.
6. S. F. Tomajczyk, *To Be a U.S. Marine* (St Paul, Minn.: Zenith Press, 2004), p. 54.

Chapter Nine   *Risks and Rewards of Being a Marine*

1. Bergen Evens, ed., *Dictionary of Quotations* (New York: Wings Books, 1993), p. 736.
2. S. F. Tomajczyk, *To Be a U.S. Marine* (St Paul, Minn.: Zenith Press, 2004), p. 135.
3. Scott Keller, *Marine Pride* (New York: Kensington Publishers, 2004), opening page.
4. Evens, p. 734.
5. Edwin Howard Simmons, ed., *The Marines* (Quantico, Va.: Marine Corps Heritage Foundation, 1998), p. 351.

anonymous—An unnamed person, usually a writer.

boot camp—Marine basic training (usually a three-month course) given to all Marine enlisted men and women.

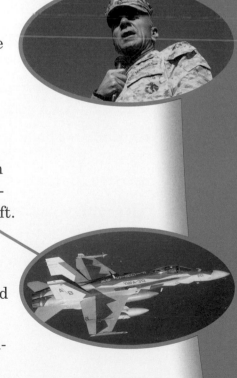

carnage—Excessive gore or pain.

chaotic—Extremely confusing.

commandant—The chief Marine, usually a four-star general.

contingent—A small military unit.

dedicate—To present a monument or a statue in a public ceremony.

elite—Superior, better than the others.

escalate—To increase or grow greater; the term was often used to describe how the Vietnam War expanded year-by-year.

ethnic groups—Groups of people based on their nationalities.

fixed-wing aircraft—Any airplane with a fixed or standard wing; helicopters having rotating wings are not fixed-wing craft.

glare—To look at or stare intensely.

infiltrator—One who approaches an enemy by taking care not to be recognized or noticed.

memoir—A written account of an experience.

mutiny—The act of forcibly taking over a ship.

OCS (Officer Candidate School)—Boot camp for officers; the officers basic training course.

prefix—A syllable in front of a word that alters that word.

proclaimed—Announced with great fanfare.

rebuff—To deny or disagree.

reluctantly—To act slowly, without commitment.

repress—To quell or restrain.

robotic—Machine-driven aircraft or ground vehicles.

ship over—Marine slang for reenlisting.

static—Stable, unmoving.

symbolize—To represent an object with another object, as a flag represents a nation.

tsunami—The massive tidal wave that swept over Pacific countries in 2004; the Marines assisted thousands of tsunami victims.

Vietcong—Vietnamese resistance fighters who fought Americans in the Vietnam War.

zealot—A person pursuing a cause with excessive enthusiasm.

Anderson, Christopher J. *The Marines in World War II: From Pearl Harbor to Tokyo Bay*. Philadelphia: Chelsea House Publishers, 2002.

Benson, Michael. *The U.S. Marine Corps*. Minneapolis: Lerner Publications, 2005.

Bradley, James with Ron Powers. *Flags of Our Fathers: Heroes of Iwo Jima*. Adapted for young people by Michael French. New York: Delacorte Press, 2001.

Green, Michael and Gladys Green. *Assault Amphibian Vehicles: The AAVs*. Mankato, Minn.: Capstone Press, 2004.

———. *Super Cobra Attack Helicopters: The AH-1W*. Mankato, Minn.: Capstone Press, 2005.

Hansen, Ole Steen. *The EA-6B Prowler*. Mankato, Minn.: Capstone Press, 2006.

Hargrove, Julia. *Marine Corps Memorial*. Carthage, Ill.: Teaching & Learning Co., 2003.

Keeter, Hunter. *The U.S. Marine Corps*. Milwaukee: World Almanac Library, 2005.

Kennedy, Robert C. *Life in the Marines*. New York: Children's Press, 2000.

Lurch, Bruno. *United States Marine Corps*. Chicago, Ill.: Heinemann Library, 2004.

Mason, Andrew. *The Vietnam War: A Primary Source History*. Milwaukee: Gareth Stevens Pub., 2006.

Olsen, Stephen P. *The Attack on U.S. Marines in Lebanon on October 23, 1983*. New York: Rosen Publishing Group, 2003.

Santella, Andrew. *Navajo Code Talkers*. Minneapolis: Compass Point Books, 2004.

Sweetman, Bill. *Jump Jets: The AV-8B Harriers*. Mankato, Minn.: Capstone High-Interest Books, 2002.

Voeller, Edward. *U.S. Marine Corps Special Forces: Recon Marines*. Mankato, Minn.: Capstone Books, 2000.

United States Marine Band
<http://www.marineband.usmc.mil>

United States Marine Corps
<http://www.usmc.mil/>

**United States Marine Corps:
Recruiting Web Site**
<http://www.marines.com/>

Index

Index